TAKE-CHARGE
SALES MANAGEMENT

TAKE-CHARGE SALES MANAGEMENT

SUCCESSFUL FIRST-YEAR STRATEGIES FOR THE NEWLY APPOINTED SALES MANAGER

Mack Hanan

Howard Berrian

James Cribbin

Jack Donis

 A Division of American Management Associations

Library of Congress Cataloging in Publication Data
Main entry under title:
HANAN, Mack et al.
Take-charge sales management.

Includes bibliographical references and index.
1. Sales management. I. Hanan, Mack.
HF5438.4.T34   658.8'1   76-22183
ISBN 0-8144-5417-8

Fifth Printing

To all the
newly appointed
field sales managers
we have taught

who, in turn,
have taught us
why they are
the single best hope
for improved professionalism
in sales

Contents

Congratulations!
You're vulnerable

When a salesman is newly appointed to management in one company we know on the *Fortune* 500 list, he receives a telegram from the president. "Congratulations," it says. "You're vulnerable." It seems to us that this says it all. In just one word, the salesman's entire past achievement is acknowledged for what it is: history. Thereafter, it will be ignored. All that will count is what he has done lately. That's where he is vulnerable. Vulnerable, in fact, is every newly appointed sales manager's middle name.

To be appointed sales manager is a salesman's opportunity of a lifetime. What can happen to wipe it out? A new sales manager can be unusually bright, work exceptionally hard, be well liked, and seemingly have everything going for him. Yet he can fail because he doesn't have his priorities straight. Knowing what to do first, and doing it, is the key we have found to successful sales management. This is what we mean by *taking charge.*

From the day of your appointment, you have about 200 working days, gain or lose a few, to take charge. That's not much to make the transition from being managed to managing, from selling to managing other men and women who sell. It may not be long enough to tell whether you will make it big. But it is every bit long enough to tell whether you will make it at all.

Making it means beating the expectation that, in moving you up, your company has traded off a good salesperson for a mediocre manager. If our experience means anything at all, we believe that there are five handles you must grasp in your first 200 days if you are going to achieve success in sales management—and convince your own managers that you will. We say *five* not because there is any magic in the number between four and six but for a couple of sound reasons. Five is graspable. You can manage five strategies at once. If you try to do many more than that, or many less, you can end up doing nothing. Five is sufficient, if they are the right five. We believe that these are. If you can take charge of the big five strategies we have in mind, you will be in control of the smallest number of prime working tools for beginning to manage a district, region, or territory from scratch.

Barring exceptions which may make your company or your own specific situation unique, we are tempted to say that if you take charge of the big five strategies and do everything else a good deal less well, you will be able to make it big. We're not encouraging you to do everything else less well, you understand. We're saying that mastering the big five strategies should be your first priority and that one of the chief rules for every new manager, along with "Watch your margins," is "Watch your priorities."

What are the big five management strategies? The first one has to do with your adoption of a take-charge leadership style. You must take leadership at once if you are going to take charge of your new managerial role. Then you must

2

make your sales growth plan, which is really your blueprint for management. In order to plan on a bottom-line basis you need to know the fundamental financial strategies of managing your volume, your costs, and your profits. Once you control a working knowledge of these skills, you are ready to manage your salesforce for its maximum profit contribution and to begin to develop its capabilities.

Each of these strategies is under your control. You can do something about them because they focus on the three variables you can affect directly and continually: your style, your plan, and your salesforce. You can affect yourself, and we are urging you to move into management quickly with a take-charge leadership posture. You can affect your sales plan, and we are suggesting that you plan to grow sales based on a written plan that is built around serving the major needs of your heavy-user customers. And you can affect your salesforce, so we are counseling you on how to manage, evaluate, and support the members of the salesforce you inherit and how to teach them the skills that can help improve their performance within your first 200 days.

When you have completed your first 200 days as sales manager, we hope you will make a discovery. The big five strategies in this book are not simply helpful in the short run to get you through the crunch. They go far beyond that. They will be crucial in seeing you all the way through to achieving your ultimate personal and career objectives. This is because they are central to the sales management process, not today's fads or just the contents of a survival kit. If you incorporate them into your management pattern now, at the very outset, you will have a head start in professionalizing them year after year as you go on. This will not only make you a good manager. It will make you a good groomer of your management successors and a principal candidate for the next moves up from your present position. Perhaps most important, your knowledge of how to apply the big five strategies will enable you to make the most powerful contribution to achieving the main objective of your company's sales function: to become as necessary to your customers as they become profitable to you.

I
How
to
take
leadership

1
How to choose
a leadership pattern

How can you become a take-charge leader? You become a leader when your salespeople permit you to do so. They are the masters. Only when your salespeople allow you to influence their thinking, their attitudes, and their behavior can you lead them. Leadership is much more a matter of what you do and what you are than it is a matter of holding the title of sales manager. Your job as leader is to release the potential of your followers. Unless they perceive you as capable of helping them satisfy their most important needs and willing to do so, and unless they look to you for guidance and direction, you will merely be their boss and not their leader.

THE FOUR FACTORS OF MANAGEMENT LEADERSHIP

Management and *leadership* are two related but distinctly separate ideas. Every sales organization needs effective management. Being an outstanding leader will not make up for your deficiencies in management. Weak managers rarely lead strong organizations.

Your objective is to be an effective manager while also being an effective leader. *Management leadership* combines these two ideas. It integrates the achievement of your organizational objectives with the satisfaction of the needs and wants of the salespeople who can make your organization successful. Therefore, you have two objectives. You want your organization to be efficient. This is a management problem. You also want the people who make your organization more efficient to get satisfaction from their efforts. This is leadership. Since you are interested in adopting the best possible leadership pattern, how can you go about it? There are four factors which you must take into account.

The first factor of leadership is *personality*. Some personality traits seem to be common denominators in all leaders. Leaders are more intelligent than others, they like to direct others, they know where they are going, they have good strategies for getting there, their social skills are good, and they like to be dominant while avoiding the extreme of being domineering.

There is no way you can change your psychological history. So instead of trying to reform yourself, ask some searching questions that will improve your personal understanding: What kind of personality characteristics do I have going for me? What are my assets? How can I get more mileage out of these positive traits than I have in the past? What limitations are hindering my effectiveness? What are my strategies for overcoming these limitations? What irremediable deficiencies do I have, and how can I prevent them from interfering with my efforts to lead people?

The second factor of leadership is *behavior*. To understand your behavior, ask these questions: What kinds of behavior on my part arouse the interest and enthusiasm of my salespeople? What makes them feel better motivated to do a more effective job? What kinds of behavior on my part tend to make them angry, annoyed, or resistant? What do I do that causes them to be unresponsive and apathetic? What do I do that gets a positive, energetic response from them?

The third leadership factor you must examine is *situation.* All leadership is situational. Each leader takes his cues not merely from what he wants but from the realities with which he must deal. A leadership pattern that is perfect with one group of salespeople may be a dismal failure with another group.

The fourth factor you must examine is *philosophy of leadership.* Ultimately your leadership will be dominated by your values, attitudes, and assumptions regarding your fellow men.

SEVEN KINDS OF LEADERSHIP

There are seven basic kinds of leader. One is the *autocratic leader* who uses and abuses his people because he has little or no respect for them. He sees them as objects to be pushed around at his whim and not as unique human beings.

Then there is the *paternalistic leader.* He sees his people as children to be protected and sheltered. He likes to have people depend on him and be emotionally tied to his apron strings. Little does he realize that his variety of leadership will dwarf their efforts and frustrate their growth and development.

At the other extreme is the *laissez-faire leader,* a weak organizational nonentity. He lets his people do pretty much as they wish even if they hurt not only the organization but themselves.

The *directive leader* has the best interests of the organization and his people at heart. He is forceful and objectives-oriented, and he wants the best job possible. But at times he forgets that people want to be led rather than driven.

The *bureaucratic leader* doesn't feel secure unless he is bolstered by rules and procedures. Everything must be done by the book. As a result, his followers spend their time on busy work, leaving little scope for imagination or creativity.

The *consultative leader* assumes that his people know some things better than he does. Therefore, he encourages their ideas. He consults with them, and, when he is capable of helping them, he eases their efforts to do a better job. He interacts with them without losing their respect because he wants to build them into a team.

Finally, the *participative leader* offers his people frequent opportunities to take part in making decisions or planning courses of action.

What is the difference between a good leader and a great leader? It is simply this: A good leader creates in his salesforce a sense of confidence in himself. A great leader creates in his salespeople a sense of confidence in *themselves.*

Most of us believe that we are natural leaders. Most of us also believe that we can pick a leader out of a crowd with unfailing success. Management leadership has attracted as many myths as realities. Take the test in Figure 1-1 to see how realistic your own concepts of leadership are. Then check your answers with Figure 1-2.

EFFECTIVE AND INEFFECTIVE
LEADERSHIP CHARACTERISTICS

Rensis Likert[1] has made a contribution to your ability to take charge quickly as a leader. In his studies of effective and ineffective leaders, he has found two differentiating characteristics: concern for production and concern for people.

Production-oriented supervisors maximize the importance of productivity, treating people as machines for getting the work out. People-oriented supervisors emphasize the need for high productivity but treat people as human beings. They are supportive rather than coercive, collaborative rather than punitive, helpful rather than driving, humane rather than harsh in their dealings with people. Four factors have been revealed in these studies.

1. *Role definition.* The production-oriented supervisor

[1]Rensis Likert, *The Human Organization* (New York: McGraw-Hill, 1967).

Figure 1–1
Management leadership myths and realities.

	TRUE	FALSE
1. Leadership and management are two related but distinct concepts.	___	___
2. Leaders tend to have personality traits different from those of their followers.	___	___
3. Leaders who are domineering and coercive fail to get high production.	___	___
4. Leaders keep a certain social distance between themselves and their people.	___	___
5. Leadership is basically the possession of a certain constellation of personality traits.	___	___
6. Negative leadership, which emphasizes strict rules and punishments, can stimulate high production.	___	___
7. Leaders almost always consult with their people regarding the proper course of action because everyone likes to participate in making decisions.	___	___
8. Leaders are generally more intelligent than their followers.	___	___
9. A company competes as much by the quality of its sales leadership as by its products.	___	___
10. Leaders are born, not developed.	___	___
11. All people can be divided into two groups: those who tend to assume leadership roles and those who tend to adopt followership roles.	___	___
12. Each leader, in his own way, likes to be dominant.	___	___

sees his role as being a pusher of work. His more successful counterpart sees his role as encouraging superior work from his people by working with and through them.

2. *Closeness of supervision.* The production-oriented supervisor acts like a one-man Gestapo, constantly checking up on his people. The people-oriented supervisor tells his

Figure 1–2
Answers to management leadership myths and realities.

1. **True.**
2. **False.** Leaders tend to have more of the same or similar traits.
3. **False.** Such leaders often get very high production, but only for the short term and often at the expense of motivation, morale, and team spirit.
4. **True.** Leaders must interact with their people but must always draw a fine line which says they cannot be "one of the boys."
5. **False.** There's more to leadership than traits.
6. **True.** Motivation, morale, and team spirit may be sacrificed.
7. **False.** Some leaders do not care for consultative management approaches. Additionally, some situations either do not require consultation or do not allow time for consultation.
8. **True.** This is a consistent truth.
9. **True.** Without the right kind of leadership, the people making, selling, and servicing products cannot achieve their best success.
10. **False.** Everyone has some leadership potential. All inborn traits can be developed to some extent.
11. **False.** A leader in one situation may be a follower in another.
12. **True.** He may be dominant in only a subtle and indirect way, but he still likes to be dominant.

---

people what is expected of them, helps them in time of need, gives them enough freedom to perform, lets them know how they will be evaluated, and then checks periodically to see to it that the work is done.

3. *Group relations.* The poor supervisor either becomes one of the boys or, more often, acts as though he lives in a different world. The good supervisor interacts with his people without allowing them to forget that he is the leader.

4. *Management history.* Autocratic supervisors have generally worked for authoritarian bosses. Effective supervisors are more likely to have worked for managers who were more collaborative and supportive.

Likert has also developed a theory of four systems of management:

1. Exploitative authoritative management, which uses and abuses employees.

2. Benevolent authoritative management, which is paternalistic.
3. Consultative management, which is characterized by interaction and reciprocal influence between the manager and his people.
4. Participative management, which is characterized by shared leadership and high levels of involvement and contribution by subordinates.

Along with Likert, many others have tried to find out what makes a leader tick. In the course of their work, two other dimensions of leadership have emerged. *Structure* involves the need for the manager to plan, organize, and control the organization and its people so that work gets done in the most efficient manner. *Consideration* involves much more than calling a man by his first name or occasionally patting him on the back. It connotes a rapport between the manager and his people based on shared trust, two-way communication, and a determined effort to help them satisfy some of their important needs and wants.

There are two other interesting aspects of consideration as it affects the tightness or looseness of organization structure: First, if consideration is high, then structure can also be high and there will be few grievances. Second, if consideration is low, increasing the structure does not seem to do much good. People either get rebellious or become ingenious at outwitting the structure. On the other hand, lowering the degree of structure does no good either. It tends to cause subordinates to have contempt for what they see as a weak leader.

Three additional aspects of leadership are also important for you to keep in mind:

1. *Maintenance of membership:* Leadership behavior and a management style that is acceptable to the workforce.
2. *Attainment of objectives:* Leadership activities geared to the efficient attainment of organizational objectives.
3. *Group interaction:* Leadership activities oriented to building a cohesive team that is committed to superior work and high morale.

For over two decades, Fred Fiedler[2] has been studying the differences between effective and ineffective leaders. He has come up with three helpful guidelines to choosing a leadership pattern.

1. *Leader-member relations.* The well-respected and well-liked leader can operate in a different manner from one who is neither liked nor respected. He can be directing, controlling, and assertive, or he can be quite permissive and democratic. The simple reason is that he has "won his wings" with his people, and they are ready to follow him and heed his efforts to guide them.

On the other hand, the disliked and disrespected manager must always be controlling, directive, and forceful because he has no other resources. Besides, his people expect it of him.

2. *Task structure.* By this, Fiedler refers to the extent to which work is structured "by the numbers." The more work that can be automatically programmed, the more likely that technology will govern the work pace and dampen the warmth and richness of the interchange that takes place between a leader and his people.

3. *Position power.* The more power the manager has, the less he must be concerned about human relations.

Fiedler asks an interesting question: "What can be done with a manager who is less than desirably effective?" For one thing, we can try to change his personality. This is usually a fruitless task. For another, we can try to put him in a job which fits his personality. This is not always possible. Or we can change the three factors noted earlier—that is, give him a job that is highly structured, give him a group he can relate to, or give him more position power.

The ideal situation is to be a well-liked leader, dealing with a highly structured situation in which you have great power. The worst situation is to be a disliked and rejected leader, dealing with a poorly structured situation and having little or no position power.

[2]Fred Fiedler, *A Theory of Leadership Effectiveness* (New York: McGraw-Hill, 1967).

Abraham Zaleznik[3] is another student of leadership. He believes that your experiences as both a leader and a follower, combined with your unique psychological history and personality constellation, predispose you to adopt one of three leadership styles.

1. *The person-oriented manager.* This leader enjoys people, likes to interact with them, and gets much-needed satisfaction from being with them. He is good at maintenance behavior—behavior that enables an organization to keep on an even keel. Accordingly, he is like an organizational gyroscope, keeping good human relations and harmony balanced within the organization.

2. *The task-oriented manager.* This leader imposes his will. He derives most of his satisfaction from achieving and is not overly concerned whether people like him or not.

3. *The fusion-oriented manager.* This leader is good at dealing with people. He can work energetically while taking his people's feelings into account.

What does it all add up to so far as you are concerned? This overview should at least purge from your mind any hope of finding a simplified approach to adopting an appropriate leadership pattern. It should give you some idea of the most important factors involved and it should remind you that leadership is based on the idea that it all depends. Effective sales leadership is dependent on the following factors.

Your salespeople. What leadership style are they used to? What has been their experience with other managers? What are their expectations of you? What are their tender nerves? What behavior do they respond well to? What behavior tends to make them feel up tight? How do they see you as their leader? Why? What can you do to change or reinforce these perceptions?

Your personality. You cannot be all things to all people. What do you have going for you? How can you capitalize more fully on your strong points? What are your remediable defects? How can you go about remedying them? What are

[3] Abraham Zaleznik, *Human Dilemmas of Leadership* (New York: Harper & Row, 1966).

your unchangeable deficiencies? How can you prevent them from undoing you?

Leadership behavior. Do you use the same leadership behavior with all your salespeople? If you do, what results are you getting? How do you try to lead? What positive and negative results are you getting? What can you do to get even better results?

Your situation. Do you have high or low sales productivity from your better people? Are your people highly motivated or content to do a so-so job? Are you planning to grow rapidly? Situational factors such as these can have an important effect on the leadership pattern you should think of adopting.

SELF-EVALUATION FOR LEADERSHIP

Leadership is not easy. That is why there are so few genuine leaders. Even the self-evaluation you must make to understand your own capacity for leadership and your preferred leadership style is difficult. Use the rating format in Figure 1-3 to give yourself practice in auditing your positive and negative characteristics. Then use the motivation–demotivation self-analysis in Figure 1-4 to gain insight into how your leadership drives can affect you and your salesforce. When you have completed both of these exercises in improving your understanding of yourself as a leader, complete your personal program for leadership along the lines of the plan shown in Figure 1-5.

Figure 1–3
Self-evaluation of leadership capacity and style.

As I rate myself: Positive Characteristics	STRONG POINT	AVERAGE POINT	WEAK POINT
1. _____	____	____	____
2. _____	____	____	____
3. _____	____	____	____
4. _____	____	____	____

5. _____	___	___	___
6. _____	___	___	___
7. _____	___	___	___
8. _____	___	___	___
9. _____	___	___	___
10. _____	___	___	___

Negative Characteristics	RARELY PRESENT	SOMETIMES PRESENT	OFTEN PRESENT
1. _____	___	___	___
2. _____	___	___	___
3. _____	___	___	___
4. _____	___	___	___
5. _____	___	___	___

As I Think My Salesforce Would Rate Me:

Positive Characteristics	STRONG POINT	AVERAGE POINT	WEAK POINT
1. _____	___	___	___
2. _____	___	___	___
3. _____	___	___	___
4. _____	___	___	___
5. _____	___	___	___
6. _____	___	___	___
7. _____	___	___	___
8. _____	___	___	___
9. _____	___	___	___
10. _____	___	___	___

Figure 1-3 (continued)

Negative Characteristics	RARELY PRESENT	SOMETIMES PRESENT	OFTEN PRESENT
1. _____	___	___	___
2. _____	___	___	___
3. _____	___	___	___
4. _____	___	___	___
5. _____	___	___	___

Figure 1-4
Self-analysis of motivation and demotivation for leadership.

1. The things that motivate me to do the best job possible are (include such things as drive to achieve and succeed, need for power, desire to be admired and respected, money, self-growth, and reputation):

   1.1. _____

   1.2. _____

   1.3. _____

   1.4. _____

   1.5. _____

   1.6. _____

2. My plan for capitalizing more fully on these motivations is:

   2.1. _____

   _____

   _____

   _____

2.2. _____

_____

_____

_____

3. The aspects of my management style that tend to demotivate my salesforce are:

   3.1. _____

   3.2. _____

   3.3. _____

   3.4. _____

4. My plan to prevent demotivation is:

   4.1. _____

_____

_____

_____

   4.2. _____

_____

_____

_____

   4.3. _____

_____

_____

_____

   4.4. _____

_____

_____

_____

Figure 1–5
Personal leadership plan.

1. My three outstanding leadership assets as a sales manager are:

   1.1. _____

   1.2. _____

   1.3. _____

   My personal program for capitalizing even more fully on my leadership assets is:

   _____

   _____

   _____

   _____

2. My three most important leadership deficiencies seem to be:

   2.1. _____

   2.2. _____

   2.3. _____

   My personal program for eliminating, or at least minimizing, my leadership deficiencies is:

   _____

   _____

   _____

   _____

2
How to perceive
salesforce needs

Up to now, you have examined your management style and your leadership pattern. Now it is appropriate to examine your process of perception of your salesforce.

Perception is one of the most puzzling problems for a new sales manager. It is full of pitfalls. Ask yourself these questions: Why do you perceive your salespeople as you do? Why do they perceive you as they do? How can you learn to perceive yourself and them more accurately? How can you get them to perceive you as you want to be perceived?

Why does misperception cause so much trouble in salesforce relations? Perception is not like the operation of a camera, which merely registers whatever happens to be out there.

It is more like the back-and-forth action of a tennis match. How I perceive you is largely a function of how you perceive me. How can you act so that your salespeople will act toward you as you want them to because their perceptions are accurate?

PRINCIPLES OF PERCEPTION

There are 14 principles of perception which have important implications for you in your role as a newly appointed sales manager.

1. Perception is extremely personal. You tend to perceive what you need to perceive. Your own inner needs determine what you perceive when you interact with your salespeople.

2. Perception is an individual process. Every person has his own rules for perceiving. What seems important to you may seem relatively unimportant to your salespeople. Some of them may be impressed by your physical appearance and other externals, whereas others are more inclined to admire your intellectual ability or some other constellation of traits.

3. Perception is a form of human transaction. How you perceive a salesman has much to do with how he perceives you. Not only does perception involve an interaction. It is also a reciprocal process. If you see a salesman as a loser, he is likely to take an equally dim view of you. This often leads to misunderstanding in a kind of ''reign of error.''

4. Perception is always selective. You cannot attend to all the cues your salesforce sends you. You must sift out those which you consider to be important. This can lead to two problems:

   4.1. Selective inattention: A tendency to ignore cues you believe to be inconsequential even though they may be crucial for understanding the other person.

   4.2. Selective sensitivity: A tendency to zero in on cues that you feel to be significant even though they may actually be insignificant.

These two tendencies may cause you to tune in or tune out the wrong cues.

5. Perception always follows the laws of economics. In sizing up a salesman, you are inclined to sort the cues he sends you in order to get as much useful information as possible in the briefest time. This may cause you to miss very important cues.

6. Perception seeks stability. In what psychologists call your strain for consistency, you tend to keep your perceptions consistent even in the face of strong countervailing evidence.

7. Perception is situational. Everything and everyone you perceive is seen within a given context or background. This background plays an important role in how you perceive.

8. A way of perceiving is, at the same time, a way of not perceiving. Once you perceive a salesman in one way, it is hard to perceive him from a different point of view.

9. We all have an implicit theory of personality that governs the traits we believe should go together. Every sales manager has his own views regarding how his people should act and what characteristics they should possess. Moreover, when a salesman shows that he possesses a given trait, his manager will tend to attribute to him other related traits that he may not actually possess. This process of trait linkage can often get you into trouble. If a salesperson is helpful to you, you are likely to assume that he is also smart and professional. On the other hand, if he is deliberate and careful, you may attribute to him such qualities as being short on self-confidence, unsure of himself, or lacking in the forcefulness that your implicit theory of personality dictates a sales representative ought to have.

10. Perceptions are often self-fulfilling prophecies. A self-fulfilling prophecy is a sometimes erroneous initial judgment which you will thereafter seek to validate by perceiving only the actions and qualities that confirm your first impression. As a result, you conclude that you were right in the first place. How could it be otherwise? This tendency leads to two other important facts about perception:

10.1. The rule of primacy: First impressions tend to be lasting. They also tend to be erroneous.

10.2. The rule of steering: First impressions serve a gating function. They tend to govern what you later perceive, maximizing what you want to see and screening out whatever you do not want to see.

11. Perception is based on your readiness to perceive. If your mind-set prepares you to see a salesman as lazy or sloppy, you will perceive all sorts of evidence of these traits. On the other hand, if your mind-set prompts you to see a salesman as doing a pretty good job, you will notice many examples of excellence in his behavior. Your readiness to perceive is closely related in these instances to the concept of self-fulfilling prophecy.

12. The managerial role you play often governs how you perceive. How do you feel that the way you play your role as manager affects how you look upon your salespeople and how they perceive you?

13. Perception is often based on irrelevant cues. This is known as the halo effect and stereotyping. You may be very impressed with a salesman who comes on like gang busters, exuding self-confidence even though he is rather incompetent and has little product knowledge or sensitivity to people. On the other hand, you may underestimate a salesman simply because he does not fit your stereotype of how a salesman should act.

14. There is often a vicious circle between perception and emotion. Some perceptions arouse your emotions, positive or negative. These emotions tend to distort your perceptions. The distorted perceptions, in turn, tend to further arouse your emotions. If you mistakenly perceive a salesman as being crafty, you will dislike him. This dislike will in turn cause you to look for more evidence that will confirm your initial dislike. When you find it, you will dislike him even more.

SUGGESTIONS FOR IMPROVING YOUR PERCEPTION

1. *Be wary of your first impressions.* Because first impressions are likely to be both lasting and wrong, it is very difficult to perceive a sales representative from a different point of view once you have passed judgment on him. Train yourself to wait until you have sufficient evidence to make a prudent judgment.

2. *Be on guard against the halo effect.* This is a tendency to judge a salesperson's individual traits through the filter of a general impression that the person has made on you. Halo may be positive or negative. Well-liked sales managers are generally judged by their staffs to be more intelligent than disliked managers. Negative halo allows a general negative impression about a person to color all your future perceptions. A sales representative who is deliberate may be misperceived as slow moving and dimwitted; or one who is reserved may be misperceived as shy and introverted.

3. *Safeguard yourself against projection.* There are two kinds of projection. The first consists of traits you do not like in yourself that you always see immediately in others. You take your own undesirable traits and project them. The second kind of projection involves blaming someone else for your errors. An ineffective sales manager typically complains that his salespeople are no good.

4. *Watch out for your perceptual defenses.* When you discover a new way of doing things, you can react in three ways. First, you can simply ignore it and shut off new knowledge. Second, you can distort it so that it fits in with your habitual perceptions. That makes it no longer new. Third, you can recognize that it doesn't conform to what you are used to and alter your perceptions to fit the new reality. This third reaction is a hallmark of good leadership.

5. *Try to avoid stereotyping.* You stereotype a salesman by judging him according to his race, religion, or nationality rather than on his merits as an individual. You deal not with the person but with his label. Stereotyping prevents you from using your mind and makes it easy for you to use your prejudices.

6. *Know yourself.* If you know your own behavior trends and tendencies, it makes it much easier to perceive others accurately. Managers who possess self-insight have a greater amount of freedom in perceiving the characteristics and traits of their salesforce. Managers who have little or no understanding of themselves are inclined to project their own tendencies on their salesforce.

7. *Be careful of your likes and dislikes.* If you like a salesman, you will perceive the ways in which he is similar

to you much more accurately than the ways in which he is dissimilar. You are also likely to underestimate the ways in which he is different. If you dislike a salesman, you will tend to focus on the things that separate you and magnify their importance rather than seeking to identify other things that you share in common.

8. *Attraction begets attraction.* In physics, opposites attract. In human relations, likes attract. If you like certain characteristics in yourself, you will tend to reject salespeople who lack them. You will also reject those who possess characteristics you dislike in yourself. On the other hand, you will be attracted to those who exhibit your own preferred traits.

9. *Be careful of your attitudes.* An attitude is a predisposition to react to a person or situation in a favorable or unfavorable manner. You react in this way even when you have little or no evidence to support your reaction. Attitudes have certain characteristics you should know about. Attitudes are learned; nobody is born with them. Furthermore, attitudes are stable and very difficult to change. Attitudes tend to be illogical. You can rarely change a salesperson's attitude simply by appealing to evidence.

Attitudes inevitably influence your perceptions and behavior. This is the subtle side of attitudes. They influence what you do even when you are not aware of them. You must be alert not only to your own attitudes but also to those of your salespeople. Otherwise, you will find yourself frustrated since your logic will rarely win out over their strongly entrenched attitudes.

SELF-ANALYSIS OF YOUR PERCEPTIVE ABILITIES AND PREFERENCES

We all believe that we see ourselves and others clearly. Yet, strangely enough, few people agree with us. Use Figure 2-1 to analyze your own perceptions about your salesforce. Then use Figure 2-2 to analyze the mutuality of the perceptions that you share with your salespeople and they share with you.

Figure 2–1
Self-analysis of perceptive abilities and preferences.

1. List five characteristics you look for in hiring a sales representative.

   1.1. _____

   1.2. _____

   1.3. _____

   1.4. _____

   1.5. _____

2. Give your reasons for looking for each of these particular characteristics.

   2.1. _____

   _____

   2.2. _____

   _____

   2.3. _____

   _____

   2.4. _____

   _____

   2.5. _____

   _____

3. Think of your best salesperson. As you perceive him, list his five strongest assets.

   3.1. _____

   _____

   3.2. _____

   _____

   3.3. _____

   _____

27

Figure 2–1 (continued)

3.4. _____

_____

3.5. _____

_____

4. Give your reasons for considering each of these qualities as being among his strongest assets.

4.1. _____

_____

4.2. _____

_____

4.3. _____

_____

4.4. _____

_____

4.5. _____

_____

5. List three traits about this same salesperson that you find most bothersome.

5.1. _____

5.2. _____

5.3. _____

6. Give your reasons for finding each of these particular traits bothersome.

6.1. _____

_____

6.2. _____

_____

6.3. _____

_____

7. Outline a program for trying to see more of this sales representative's positive traits while at the same time not allowing his negative traits to interfere with your efforts to relate to him.

_____

_____

_____

_____

_____

_____

_____

_____

Figure 2-2
Perception audit.

Select the five personal characteristics that you like most about yourself, numbering them from 1 to 5 in the rank order of their importance to you. Then rank the five traits in your makeup that you dislike most.

Things I Like Most About Myself	Things I Dislike Most About Myself
1. _____	1. _____
2. _____	2. _____
3. _____	3. _____
4. _____	4. _____
5. _____	5. _____

Now rank five things you think your salespeople like and dislike most about you. Would they rank the same items you did in the same order? If not, what might the differences be telling you

Figure 2–2 (continued)

if you want to increase the accuracy of the perceptions that exist between you?

Things I Think My Salespeople Like Most About Me	Things I Think My Salespeople Dislike Most About Me
1. _____	1. _____
2. _____	2. _____
3. _____	3. _____
4. _____	4. _____
5. _____	5. _____

I plan to improve my ability to perceive my salesforce by doing the following:

1. _____

2. _____

3. _____

4. _____

5. _____

I plan to improve my ability to perceive my salesforce by avoiding doing the following:

1. _____

2. _____

3. _____

4. _____

5. _____

3

How to motivate
your salesforce

A *motive* is anything that causes a salesperson to satisfy his needs. Some motives are internal: pride, curiosity, the desire to excel, to learn, to grow, to achieve. Other motives are external: praise, a chance for promotion, a salary increase, higher status, and more privileges. External motives are called incentives.

Motivation is the art of encouraging salespeople to do well what they might otherwise do in a slipshod manner and to do willingly what they must or ought to do.

Job satisfaction is a subjective judgment that a salesperson makes regarding the extent to which he is receiving what he thinks he has a right to receive.

Morale is a group phenomenon which has at least four characteristics: (1) a feeling of team spirit; (2) identification with group goals as a means for attaining personal objectives; (3) a sense of contributing to the achievement of the group's goals; (4) observable progress toward the goals.

Let's examine these subjects more closely. Motivation can make the difference between excellence and mediocrity. Therefore, every sales manager asks, "How can I motivate my salesforce?" The key is to pinpoint the needs that your salespeople are trying to satisfy and to help satisfy them. No tricks or gimmicks will ever substitute for this hard diagnostic process. The second step is to use some of the ideas presented by A. H. Maslow.[1]

MASLOW'S HIERARCHY OF NEEDS

According to Maslow, human needs constitute a hierarchy. At the lowest level are our *physiological* needs. Next is our need for *security*. At a higher level in this hierarchy are our needs for *affiliation*. These are social needs. At a still higher level are our *esteem needs;* we all want a certain amount of prestige, success, achievement, and status. Finally, at the very highest level is our need for *self-actualization,* our need to develop our human potential. The way you motivate your people—actually, it would be more accurate to say that you help them motivate themselves—is by recognizing their needs and providing opportunities for them to satisfy these needs. Maslow has made four additional discoveries.

1. An unsatisfied need is a motivator; a satisfied need stops being a motivator.

2. When needs at one level are relatively well satisfied, we reach out to satisfy needs that are at a higher level.

3. All needs interact, and most of them are operating most of the time. Moreover, we all want a balanced diet of need satisfaction and not just the maximization of one need.

[1] A. H. Maslow, *Motivation and Personality* (New York: Harper & Row, 1954).

4. The lower-level needs dealing with security are geared to the avoidance of pain and to survival. Higher-level needs related to self-esteem and self-actualization are geared to growth, learning, advancement, independence, success, self-respect, meaningful job recognition, and personal development.

HERZBERG'S MAINTAINERS AND SATISFIERS

Frederick Herzberg[2] has made a distinction between motivations that are *maintainers* and *satisfiers*. The maintainers are salary, job security, working conditions, fringe benefits, company policy, and administration. Maintainers have three characteristics: (1) They are incentives that usually give only short-term results. To get more productivity, you have to give more and more of them. (2) They appeal to Maslow's lower-level needs. (3) They prevent dissatisfaction; hold down gripes, complaints, and grievances; and make the work environment congenial.

Satisfiers are motivators that usually give long-term results. They make a man a self-starter. They appeal to higher-level needs in the Maslow hierarchy. Satisfiers are geared to the man himself or the job that he is doing. In contrast, maintainers are oriented to things external to the man and his job.

In your day-to-day operations, you should try to prevent demotivation by seeing to it that your people satisfy their lower-level needs and Herzberg's maintainers. Fair money rewards, good treatment, reasonable fringe benefits, constructive discipline, and security are your major working tools.

Above and beyond these fundamentals you can help your salespeople satisfy their social needs by interacting with them in a friendly way, by building up each person to the others, by helping them resolve frictions or disputes that may arise, by helping them work as a team, and by trying to build team spirit. In addition, you can help them achieve growth by new

[2] Frederick Herzberg, *Work and the Nature of Man* (Cleveland: World Publishing Co., 1966).

learning. You can also give them a certain amount of freedom to use their own ideas and talents. Listen to their suggestions and their legitimate complaints. Consult with them on planning, problem solving, and decision making.

Perhaps most important of all, you can help your people recognize that they are doing meaningful work. Try to motivate them through the job itself. This is *job enrichment*. The essential idea in job enrichment is to give each sales representative a greater share of personal responsibility. Instead of spending most of his time reacting to the demands and orders of others, job enrichment provides opportunities for him to act on his own.

Most salespeople want challenging work, competent, fair, and supportive supervision, a chance to get ahead, fair pay and fringe benefits, credit for a job well done, and reasonably open communication. They also tend to look for fair discipline, training and development, and increasing challenge. Now consider these questions: How much of each of these factors do your salespeople get from their work? What can you do to insure a balanced ration of each of these motivating factors? How can you capitalize on good morale to channel it into higher productivity and satisfaction? The following suggestions will help:

—Build a climate of cooperation which prompts sales-people to help one another.
—Prevent friction by clearly defining job responsibilities in the areas of accountability and freedom.
—Increase the stature of each sales representative in the eyes of his peers and customers.
—Serve as a mediator helping resolve disputes and fric-tions.
—Seek out opportunities to interact with your salespeople on a cordial and supportive basis.
—Reward their efforts in personal as well as professional ways.

It is very important that you set an example by working with your people rather than merely having them work for you. You can help them understand not only what they must do but why they should do it and why it should be done well.

Encourage your salesforce to exchange suggestions and constructive criticisms and to formulate improved and innovative ways of doing the job.

AVOIDING DEMOTIVATION

Just as you can motivate your salespeople, you can also demotivate them. Here's how.

—Be sarcastic. Never enhance a man. Seek out opportunities to make him feel small.

—Ignore constructive criticisms, suggestions, and honest questions.

—Run a one-man show and never allow your salespeople to influence you. If they make an impression on you, don't let them know it.

—Be indecisive and weak. Never communicate.

—Play favorites. Have special friends and enemies. Take it out on those you dislike.

—Accept all credit when things go right. Throw all the blame to your salespeople when things go wrong.

—Be a manipulator and a schemer.

—Be obviously unethical.

—Be a boaster, always talking about I, me, and mine.

Herzberg believes that the following things are true: (1) Many of the actions that managers think motivate salespeople do not really motivate them. (2) Some of the rewards that we often think of as motivators are simply maintainers. They serve to meet low-level needs, hold down complaints, and prevent dissatisfaction. If they are not present in reasonable amounts, salespeople will be demotivated. But they do not motivate. Herzberg has identified a different set of factors as motivators. In other words, Herzberg is saying that two different sets of factors are necessary: the maintainers to help prevent dissatisfaction and the satisfiers or motivators to create positive motivation that stimulates a better job. This is the way he aligns each set of factors.

MAINTAINERS	SATISFIERS
1. Salary	1. Achievement
2. Job security	2. Earned recognition
3. Job status	3. The work itself
4. Company policy and administration	4. Increased responsibility
5. Working conditions	5. Advancement
6. Fringe benefits	6. Growth
7. Manager's competence	

Use Figure 3-1* to check the extent to which you are using each maintainer and satisfier to move your salesforce. Then, on the basis of what your analysis reveals, use Figures 3-2 and 3-3 to plan how you will improve your methods for helping your salespeople motivate themselves and upgrade their job satisfaction. These steps will act to improve salesforce morale. Morale is a group phenomenon. Remember that it has four characteristics: (1) a feeling of "we-ness" that those outside the group do not have; (2) an acceptance of the group's goals, coupled with a feeling that personal objectives can best be achieved by working with and through the group; (3) a feeling on the part of each member that he is making a significant contribution to the group's goals; (4) noticeable progress toward the achievement of these goals. Use Figure 3-4 to plan how you will go about improving morale in your salesforce.

THEORY X AND THEORY Y MANAGEMENT

Every manager has his own theory of management. Two prevalent theories are theory X and theory Y. Which do you subscribe to? Use Figure 3-5 to find out. First answer all 11 questions, then read on to see which category fits you better.

Both theory X and theory Y are stereotypes. Each stands

---

*All figures for this chapter have been placed at the end of the chapter.

for a set of assumptions which most managers make about themselves, their people, and work itself. Douglas McGregor[3] says that theory X management, which accords with the so-called traditional assumptions of management, tends to make the average worker compliant rather than creative and productive. Theory X management operates on the assumption that people will do only so much work as the money "carrot" and the "club" of control force them to do. Given half a chance, the average worker will goldbrick. Managers who operate under such assumptions, according to McGregor, are theory X managers.

If you agreed with most or all of the first five items in Figure 3-5, you tend to manage according to theory X. On the other hand, if you checked items 6 to 11 under the column headed "Agree," you tend to be a theory Y manager.

Theory X managers tend to engage in push-pull management behavior. Theory Y managers, on the other hand, try to gain cooperation by treating their salespeople as human beings. To a far greater extent than theory X managers, they delegate authority and responsibility, ask for suggestions, listen to ideas, and consult on what should be done when they believe that their salespeople are competent to contribute. Theory X managers, however, tend to run one-man shows. They do all the problem solving and decision making. They drive rather than lead.

THEORY Y MANAGEMENT AND JOB ENRICHMENT

If you are a theory Y manager, you will be concerned with enriching the job satisfactions of your salesforce on a daily basis. Here are some examples of job enrichment steps you can consider.

—A sales representative is allowed to keep his own performance records.

—A sales representative is given a total system of products and services to sell rather than a single product.

[3] Douglas McGregor, *The Human Side of Enterprise* (New York: Mc-Graw-Hill, 1960).

—A sales representative is given responsibility for serving a given customer segment. He has personal responsibility for satisfying "his" customers.

—A sales representative is allowed to answer letters of complaint personally.

—A sales representative gets feedback on his performance directly from you rather than through an intermediate supervisor.

—A sales representative is given greater freedom to make certain decisions that relate to his job.

—A sales representative is given authority to solve problems within his competence and responsibility without being forced to buck every decision topside to you.

—A sales representative is allowed freedom to do his job as he thinks best, is held accountable for results, and is allowed to control his own work rather than have the work control him.

Use Figure 3-6 to work out your own plan of job enrichment for your salesforce.

Figure 3–1
Maintainer and satisfier usage inventory.

Maintainers	USE RARELY	USE SOMETIMES	USE OFTEN
Physiological Needs			
Job rotation for work variety	____	____	____
Good selling tools to work with	____	____	____
Safety and Security Needs			
Fair treatment	____	____	____
Job security	____	____	____
Fair discipline	____	____	____
Reasonable rules	____	____	____
Systems for ventilating grievances	____	____	____
Fair salary and bonus	____	____	____

Social and Affiliation Needs
Friendliness   ___   ___   ___

Periodic interaction with each sales representative   ___   ___   ___

Building team spirit and morale   ___   ___   ___

Resolving conflict   ___   ___   ___

Building up one salesperson to others   ___   ___   ___

Helping to relieve tensions   ___   ___   ___

Listening to suggestions   ___   ___   ___

Holding periodic meetings   ___   ___   ___

Providing time when salespeople can speak and interact with me   ___   ___   ___

Holding parties, outings, and picnics   ___   ___   ___

	USE RARELY	USE SOMETIMES	USE OFTEN
Satisfiers			
Ego and Esteem Needs			
Earned recognition and praise for a job well done	___	___	___
Training and development of key people	___	___	___
Delegation of authority and responsibility	___	___	___
Advancement opportunities	___	___	___
Use of consultative and participative management	___	___	___
Involvement in planning and decision making	___	___	___
Opportunities for each sales representative to use full talents and skills	___	___	___

Figure 3–1 (continued)

Self-fulfillment Needs
Freedom to act and perform   ___   ___   ___

Freedom to use personal ideas   ___   ___   ___

Opportunities for each sales representative to grow on the job   ___   ___   ___

Job enrichment through greater decision-making, problem-solving, and self-determining work   ___   ___   ___

Figure 3–2
Salesforce need satisfaction plan.

1. I plan to help my salespeople satisfy their *physiological needs* more fully by:

   1.1. _____

   _____

   1.2. _____

   _____

   1.3. _____

   _____

2. I plan to help my salespeople satisfy their *safety and security needs* more fully by:

   2.1. _____

   _____

   2.2. _____

   _____

2.3. _____

_____

3. I plan to help my salespeople satisfy their *social and affiliation needs* more fully by:

3.1. _____

_____

3.2. _____

_____

3.3. _____

_____

4. I plan to help my salespeople satisfy their *ego and esteem needs* more fully by:

4.1. _____

_____

4.2. _____

_____

4.3. _____

_____

5. I plan to help my salespeople satisfy their *self-fulfillment needs* more fully by:

5.1. _____

_____

5.2. _____

_____

5.3. _____

_____

Figure 3–3
Job satisfaction improvement plan.

1. I plan to help my salespeople increase their *job satisfaction* by taking the following practical steps:

   1.1. _____

   _____

   1.2. _____

   _____

   1.3. _____

   _____

   1.4. _____

   _____

   1.5. _____

   _____

2. I plan to reduce or eliminate sources of my salespeople's *job dissatisfaction* by taking the following practical steps:

   2.1. _____

   _____

   2.2. _____

   _____

   2.3. _____

   _____

   2.4. _____

   _____

   2.5. _____

   _____

Figure 3–4
Salesforce morale improvement plan.

1. I intend to develop a feeling of *"we-ness" and team spirit* in my salespeople by taking the following practical steps:

1.1. _____

_____

1.2. _____

_____

1.3. _____

_____

2. I intend to help my salespeople accept *the goals of the organization* and achieve their *personal objectives* through working for these goals by taking the following practical steps:

2.1. _____

_____

2.2. _____

_____

2.3. _____

_____

3. I intend to help each of my salespeople realize that his work is important and that he is making *a significant contribution to our shared success* by taking the following practical steps:

3.1. _____

_____

3.2. _____

_____

3.3. _____

_____

Figure 3–4 (continued)

4. I intend to keep my salespeople informed on our *progress toward the achievement of organization goals* by taking the following practical steps:

4.1. _____

_____

4.2. _____

_____

4.3. _____

_____

Figure 3–5
Theory X and theory Y analysis.

AGREE   DISAGREE

_____   1. The average salesperson has an inherent   _____
dislike for work and will avoid it if he can.

_____   2. Because salespeople dislike work, they must   _____
be either bribed with money or coerced to perform.

_____   3. The average salesperson prefers to be direct-   _____
ed in his work and wishes to avoid responsibility.

_____   4. The average salesperson has little ambition   _____
and desires job security above all else.

_____   5. The average salesperson must be closely   _____
supervised and tightly controlled to get him to
do a good job.

_____   6. The expenditure of physical and mental effort   _____
in work is as natural as play.

_____   7. Under the right conditions, the average sales-   _____
person learns not only to accept responsibility
but to seek it.

_____   8. External controls and threats of punishment   _____
are not the only ways to get people to work for
the attainment of organizational objectives.

_____   9. Under conditions of modern business life, the   _____
intellectual abilities of the average salesperson
are only partially utilized.

_____ 10. The ability to be innovative and to come up _____
with practical improvements is widely distributed
throughout any organization and not necessarily
limited to the higher echelons.
_____ 11. The commitment of salespeople to organiza- _____
tion objectives is a function of their rewards.

Figure 3–6
Job enrichment plan.

I plan to apply the following *job enriching practices and policies*
to my salesforce on the following dates and with the following
salespeople:

Job Enrichment Policy or Practice	Date to Institute	Salespeople Applied to

II
How
to
improve
your
profit / volume
contribution

4
How to improve your turnover

The business of the territory you manage is a money machine. If you think of it this way and understand how it operates, you will be able to maximize your profit contribution.

Every strategy you implement affects your money machine. By the sales you generate, you cause cash to flow into investment in new inventories. These inventories then flow into new receivables. Finally, the receivables flow back into new cash which has accumulated an added value called *profit*. Part of this profit comes to you in the form of your salary, bonus, and other rewards. Because you generate operating funds, you have a direct effect on profit. In turn, profit has a direct effect on you.

Your company tells you to sell. This is corporate shorthand for "sell profitably." Only profitable sales make money for you and the company because only profitable sales can add to the circulating capital of your business.

Your territorial money machine runs on three principles. One is the principle of turnover, which is the way you grow the circulating capital allocated by your management to the territory you serve. The second principle is concerned with relating profit to your volume and costs so that you make money as well as sales and investments. The third principle has to do with knowing and applying the marginal contribution which each individual product or service makes to its line. By putting the principle of contribution margin to work, you can determine the emphasis you must place on selling each product, the type and number of salespeople who should be out selling it, and the dollar value of support you should use as backup for them. When you apply all three principles, you will be doing something called managing your business.

Your business, like all businesses, begins with an investment of capital. If the capital sits there or flows out, the business dies. In order for a business to live and grow, its capital must circulate. Circulating capital is made up of three components: cash, inventories, and receivables. Use Figure 4-1 to calculate the circulating capital currently allocated to your business. If you don't know the exact numbers, make an estimate. In Figure 4-2(a) you will see the start of the capital circulation process labeled as cash.

Cash is useful to your business because you can create inventories by investing it. Since inventories are the source of eventual sales, funds flowing from cash to inventories add to their value. There are three typical management actions that cause funds to flow from cash to inventories: (1) materials purchases, (2) payroll, and (3) overhead expenses. Figure 4-2b shows the step in the capital circulation process where cash flows into inventories.

Through the sales which you and your salesforce generate, the second step in the circulating capital cycle occurs when funds flow from inventories into receivables. In the process, the magnitude of the funds increases. This happens because

Figure 4–1
Circulating capital allocation.

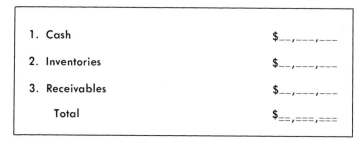

inventories are valued at cost and receivables are valued at selling price. The difference between them is gross profit. In Figure 4-2(b) you can see where gross profits are made.

Finally, as a result of sales, funds flow from receivables to cash to complete the circulating capital cycle. During this part of the cycle, the magnitude of funds in circulation is reduced by the cost of selling and administrative expenses. Figure 4-2(c) shows where this decrease occurs. In spite of this depletion, the magnitude of total funds in the system should increase. The amount of increase is called operating profit. Figure 4-2(c) shows how profit can be accumulated at the completion of each individual turn of your territory's money machine.

Since the funds which make up your circulating capital increase with each turn of the capital cycle, everything you do should be designed to maximize the rate of its turnover. One turn a year represents a turnover rate of 100 percent. If this were your current turnover rate, and you could increase it to once every three months, you would have stepped up your turnover rate 4 times to 400 percent.

Profits are made by turnover. Improving turnover improves profits. It is essential that you understand what your current turnover rate is for each product or service and that you learn how to accelerate it by applying basic business management principles. In the course of improving your product line turnover rates, you will be helping to maximize profit in two ways: You will be increasing your own territorial profit contribution, and you will be helping your management

Figure 4–2
The capital circulation process.

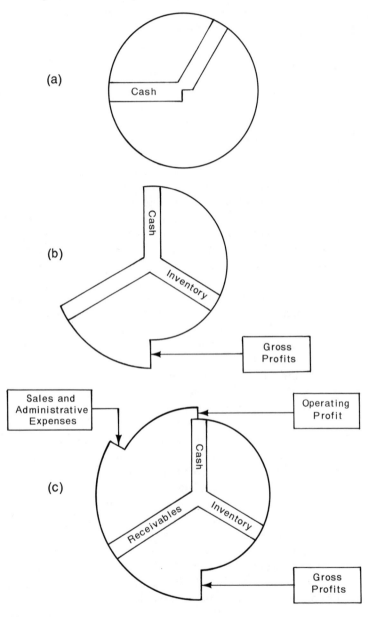

(a)

Cash

(b)

Cash

Inventory

Gross
Profits

Sales and
Administrative
Expenses

Operating
Profit

(c)

Cash

Receivables

Inventory

Gross
Profits

52

Figure 4–3
Turnover improvement plan.

PRODUCT OR SERVICE	TURNOVER RATE		TURNOVER IMPROVEMENT STRATEGY	
	CURRENT	IMPROVED TO	INCREASE SALES BY	DECREASE INVESTMENT BY

make its operating funds work harder. Use Figure 4-3 to work out the current turnover rate for each of your key products or services. Then decide which of the two ways of improving turnover you will apply to each product or service. Will you try to increase its sales or reduce its investment in total operating assets? Your decision should become the basis of your strategic plan for each product or service.

5

How to manage your volume-cost-profit relationship

Whether you are able to achieve your sales growth objectives depends on how well you understand and manage the relationship between volume and costs. These are the two major factors that affect your profit. By understanding the volume-cost interaction on profit, you will be able to predict how many units of your products or services you will have to sell, what quotas to set for them, and at what price you will have to sell them in order to reach your objectives.

CASE HISTORY IN RELATING VOLUME
AND COSTS TO PROFIT

To help you learn to relate volume and costs to profit, work out the following case history. As you go along, keep reminding yourself how these principles can apply to your own products or services.

Assume you have a new product in your line. Its first-year sales are 6,500 units. Here is your fact base:

Sales price of all units	$195,000
Average sales price per unit	30
Average variable cost per unit	20
Total variable costs of all units	130,000
Fixed costs per annum	32,000

This fact base is the platform for the exercises that follow.

The term "cost behavior" means the increase or decrease in the amount of costs incurred. There are two kinds of cost. Variable costs increase or decrease with the number of units sold. Fixed costs are time costs; they increase or decrease in relation to the time expired. Thus a monthly fixed cost of $1 will amount to $3 at the end of three months regardless of the number of units sold.

Derive a Sales Value for Volume

In Figure 5-1, enter in column 2 the sales values for each of the corresponding number of units in column 1. Use the average sales price per unit. Round your calculations to the nearest hundreds or thousands. Compare your sales values with the answers shown in Figure 5-2. Then enter in column 3 the variable costs for each number of units. Variable costs on a unit basis have a fixed relationship to selling prices. They increase and decrease by variations in volume or number of units sold. Round your calculations to the nearest hundreds or thousands.

Figure 5–1
Profits on sales: volume–cost–profit relationship.

1	2	3	4	5	6
NO. OF UNITS	SALES	VARIABLE COSTS	CONTRIBUTION MARGIN	FIXED COSTS	OPERATING PROFIT
Volume			(2 minus 3)		(5 minus 4)
0	$	$	$	$	$
1,000					
2,000					
3,000					
4,000					
5,000					
6,000					
7,000					

Figure 5–2
Profits on sales: volume–cost–profit relationship.

1	2	3	4	5	6
NO. OF UNITS	SALES	VARIABLE COSTS	CONTRIBUTION MARGIN	FIXED COSTS	OPERATING PROFIT
	Unit Price				
Volume	× Volume		(2 minus 3)		(5 minus 4)
0	$ 0	$	$	$	$
1,000	30,000				
2,000	60,000				
3,000	90,000				
4,000	120,000				
5,000	150,000				
6,000	180,000				
7,000	210,000				

Discover Contribution Margin

Compare your variable costs with the answers shown in Figure 5-3. When variable costs are subtracted from sales, the results are values generally referred to as *contribution margin.* This is the margin, or difference, between sales and variable costs that contributes to fixed costs and profit. In

Figure 5–3
Profits on sales: volume–cost–profit relationship.

1	2	3	4	5	6
NO. OF		VARIABLE	CONTRIBUTION		OPERATING
UNITS	SALES	COSTS	MARGIN	FIXED COSTS	PROFIT
	Unit Price	Unit Cost			
Volume	× Volume	× Volume	(2 minus 3)		(5 minus 4)
0	$ 0	$	$	$	$
1,000	30,000	20,000			
2,000	60,000	40,000			
3,000	90,000	60,000			
4,000	120,000	80,000			
5,000	150,000	100,000			
6,000	180,000	120,000			
7,000	210,000	140,000			

Figure 5–4
Profits on sales: volume–cost–profit relationship.

1	2	3	4	5	6
NO. OF		VARIABLE	CONTRIBUTION		OPERATING
UNITS	SALES	COSTS	MARGIN	FIXED COSTS	PROFIT
	Unit Price	Unit Cost			
Volume	× Volume	× Volume	(2 minus 3)		(5 minus 4)
0	$ 0	$ 0	$ 0	$	$
1,000	30,000	20,000	10,000		
2,000	60,000	40,000	20,000		
3,000	90,000	60,000	30,000		
4,000	120,000	80,000	40,000		
5,000	150,000	100,000	50,000		
6,000	180,000	120,000	60,000		
7,000	210,000	140,000	70,000		

Figure 5-3, enter in column 4 the contribution margin at each level of volume shown in column I. Compare your contribution margins with the answers shown in Figure 5-4. Then in column 5 of Figure 5-4, enter the fixed costs of the first year's operations of your sales growth plan for this product.

Now you can perform a simple breakeven analysis of your new product. At the point in the volume column where the contribution margin equals annual fixed costs, your operation will break even. Any volume level below this point will produce a loss. Any volume level above this point will produce a profit.

Compare your fixed costs with the answers shown in Figure 5-5. In column 6 enter the operating profits or losses for each volume level shown in column 1. Compare your operating profits or losses with the answers shown in Figure 5-6.

Once you have all the numbers shown in Figure 5-6, you can begin to visualize them in diagram form so that their meaning is evident at a glance. On Figure 5-7, use the numbers from columns 1 and 2 of Figure 5-6 to plot the sales line. Label it. Then compare your sales line with Figure 5-8.

Use Figure 5-8 to plot the variable costs line from the numbers in column 2 of Figure 5-6. Label it. Then compare your variable cost line with Figure 5-9. Notice that contribution margin shows up once again as the difference between variable costs and sales.

On Figure 5-9, add the fixed costs line. This will enable you to see how your total costs are the sum of the variable costs in column 3 of Figure 5-6 and the fixed costs in column 5. Then compare your fixed costs with Figure 5-10. Label your profit and loss in the proper triangular spaces on Figure 5-10.

The loss triangle represents unabsorbed fixed costs. The profit triangle represents the cumulative contribution margin after annual fixed costs have been absorbed.

Figure 5-11 shows where your breakeven point is located. Using the figures derived from your volume–cost–profit analysis, you can determine breakeven with this formula:

$$Q = \frac{F}{P - V}$$

where Q = units (quantity) at breakeven
F = fixed costs

Figure 5–5
Profits on sales: volume–cost–profit relationship.

1 NO. OF UNITS Volume	2 SALES Unit Price × Volume	3 VARIABLE COSTS Unit Cost × Volume	4 CONTRIBUTION MARGIN (2 minus 3)	5 FIXED COSTS	6 OPERATING PROFIT (5 minus 4)
0	$ 0	$ 0	$ 0	$32,000	$
1,000	30,000	20,000	10,000	32,000	
2,000	60,000	40,000	20,000	32,000	
3,000	90,000	60,000	30,000	32,000	
4,000	120,000	80,000	40,000	32,000	
5,000	150,000	100,000	50,000	32,000	
6,000	180,000	120,000	60,000	32,000	
7,000	210,000	140,000	70,000	32,000	

Figure 5–6
Profits on sales: volume–cost–profit relationship.

1 NO. OF UNITS Volume	2 SALES Unit Price × Volume	3 VARIABLE COSTS Unit Cost × Volume	4 CONTRIBUTION MARGIN (2 minus 3)	5 FIXED COSTS	6 OPERATING PROFIT (5 minus 4)
0	$ 0	$ 0	$ 0	$32,000	$(32,000)
1,000	30,000	20,000	10,000	32,000	(22,000)
2,000	60,000	40,000	20,000	32,000	(12,000)
3,000	90,000	60,000	30,000	32,000	(2,000)
4,000	120,000	80,000	40,000	32,000	8,000
5,000	150,000	100,000	50,000	32,000	18,000
6,000	180,000	120,000	60,000	32,000	28,000
7,000	210,000	140,000	70,000	32,000	38,000

P = sales price per unit
V = variable costs per unit

From Figure 5-6 we arrive at these values: $P = \$30$, $V = \$20$, and $F = \$32,000$. Applying the formula to this analysis results in the following breakeven:

(Please turn to page 65.)

Figure 5–7
Breakeven analysis: sales . . .

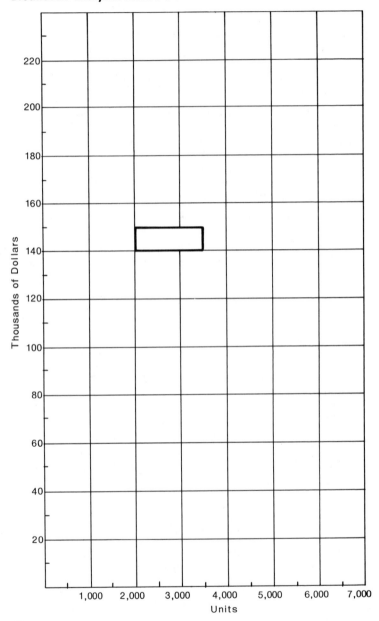

Figure 5–8
Breakeven analysis: minus variable costs . . .

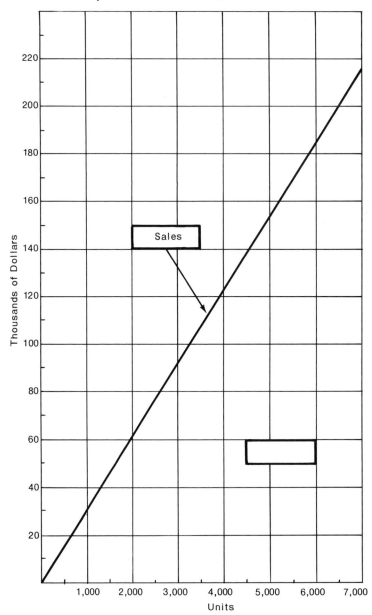

Figure 5–9
Breakeven analysis: equals contribution margin . . .

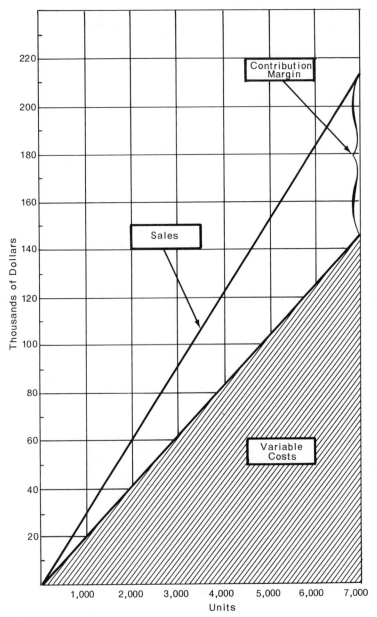

Figure 5–10
Breakeven analysis: minus fixed costs . . .

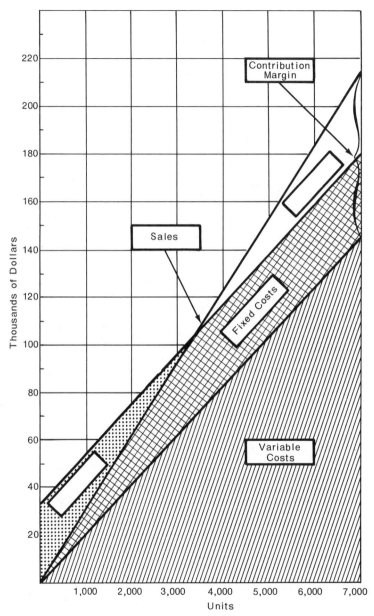

Figure 5–11
Breakeven analysis: reveals breakeven point.

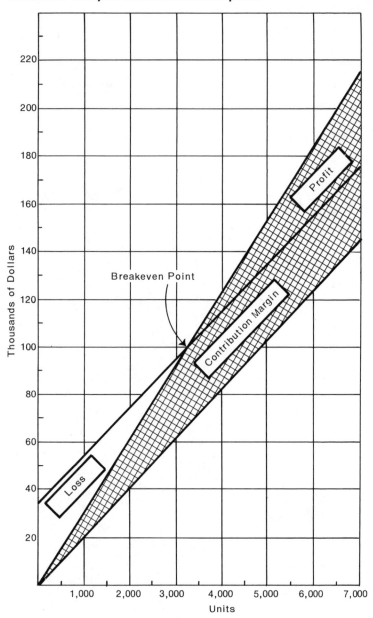

$$Q = \frac{32,000}{30 - 20}$$

$$= \frac{32,000}{10}$$

$$= 3,200 \text{ units at breakeven}$$

Breakeven analysis is a basic tool for setting sales growth objectives. It is also a key to establishing sales quotas for existing products and an important consideration for determining the profit you can expect on new products. It highlights the fixed costs you will incur from making an investment to achieve a given potential output and profit target.

RELATE VOLUME–COSTS–PROFIT TO YOUR OWN PRODUCT LINE

Now that you have practiced relating volume and costs to profit in the case history, use the same approach to your own product line.

First, work up the fact base for each of your key products or services by itemizing the following information:

1. Sales price of all units.
2. Average sales price per unit.
3. Average variable cost per unit.
4. Total variable costs of all units.
5. Fixed costs per annum.

Then use the form in Figure 5-1 as a model to discover the volume-cost-profit relationships for each product or service whose fact base you have gathered. Round your calculations to the nearest hundreds or thousands.

Next, perform a breakeven analysis of each product or service. Remember that breakeven occurs at the point in the volume column where contribution margin equals annual fixed costs. Profit can occur only at volume levels above this point. Use Figure 5-11 as a model to pinpoint the exact location where each product or service breaks even. Apply the same formula you used for breakeven analysis:

$$Q = \frac{F}{P - V}$$

Use your breakeven analysis as the platform from which to set sales growth objectives and establish sales quotas. Think of breakeven as the floor of each product's performance and ask yourself, How high above the floor can I grow this business?

6

How to manage your product line

Each product or product line, as well as each service you sell, makes its own contribution to profit. Some products make a positive contribution; they are the profit makers. A few products make the largest contribution; they are the big winners. Some products may make a negative contribution; they are the losers.

The best way to achieve your sales growth objectives is to push your big winners. By applying the contribution margin principle, you will be able to pick out your big winners. You will also know where your other products stand as profit contributors. This will help you determine priorities for allocating salesforce time and the amount of pressure you want your salesforce to apply to each item in the line. A further benefit is the insight you can gain about products or services that may be sleepers: that is, potential big winners that make a small contribution right now but may be able to generate superior profits if you feature them.

CASE HISTORY IN PRODUCT LINE MANAGEMENT

To help you learn to manage your product line, work out the following case history. As you go along with it, keep reminding yourself how these principles can apply to your own products or services.

Three-Product Profit Management

Assume you have a three-product line comprising products A, B, and C. Your fact base is shown in the accompanying table.

	PRODUCT A	PRODUCT B	PRODUCT C
Sales			
Amount	$200,000	$300,000	$200,000
Percent	100.0%	100.0%	100.0%
Variable costs	67.5	67.5	60.0
Contribution	32.5%	32.5%	40.0%
Fixed costs	$ 34,000	$ 34,000	$ 34,000

Start with the three bar graphs in Figure 6-1, headed A, B, C. Enter one product's sales figure at the bottom of each of the upper set of bar graphs. Calculate the variable costs for each product. Scale off on the upper bar graph the sales amount for each product. The remaining segment of the bar graph represents each product's contribution margin. Enter the amount and percentage of each product's contribution margin as indicated. In the lower set of bar graphs, scale off the amount of each product's contribution margin and enter the amount below each lower bar graph. Scale off the amount of fixed costs and enter the amount where it is indicated. The remaining segment of the contribution margin

Figure 6–1

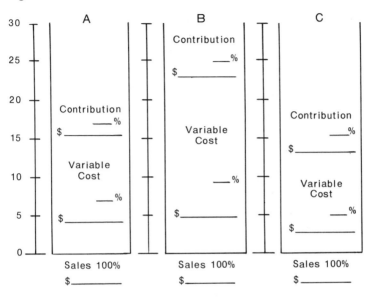

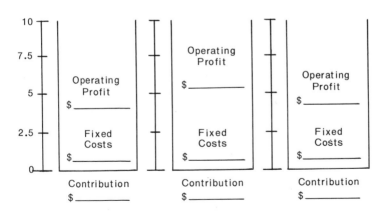

Figure 6–2

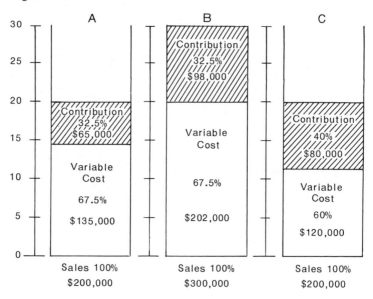

A
Contribution 32.5% $65,000
Variable Cost 67.5% $135,000
Sales 100% $200,000

B
Contribution 32.5% $98,000
Variable Cost 67.5% $202,000
Sales 100% $300,000

C
Contribution 40% $80,000
Variable Cost 60% $120,000
Sales 100% $200,000

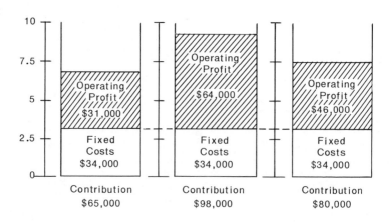

Operating Profit $31,000
Fixed Costs $34,000
Contribution $65,000

Operating Profit $64,000
Fixed Costs $34,000
Contribution $98,000

Operating Profit $46,000
Fixed Costs $34,000
Contribution $80,000

represents the operating profit of each product.

Which of the three products produces the greatest contribution margin? Which of the three products has the greatest operating profit?

As Figure 6-2 shows, product B produces the greatest contribution margin because its sales are the greatest and its 32.5% contribution margin is equal to product A. Product C has a greater contribution margin than A because its variable costs percentage is lower. Product B has the greatest operating profit because its contribution margin is the greatest. Product C has the next best operating profit because its contribution margin is greater than product A.

Two-Product Profit Management

Now assume that in another category you have only a two-product line. Assess the relative contribution to profit of product 1 sales as against product 2 sales. Enter the data required in Figure 6-3.

Sales
 Product 1 = $2,000,000
 Product 2 = 1,500,000
Variable costs:
 Product 1 = $1,400,000
 Product 2 =   750,000
Fixed costs: = $1,000,000

All these figures are expressed as annual amounts. This is because determinations of relative profit are more significant on an annual basis than for any shorter time period. Remember that variable costs increase and decrease with sales volume. Fixed costs are time costs.

Figure 6-4 is a simplified operating statement. On it, enter the required numbers for products 1 and 2 along with their totals. Round all percentages to whole numbers.

With total contribution equal to 100 percent, calculate and enter the percentage that product 1 represents of the total contribution. Do the same for the profit contribution of product 2. The sum of these two figures should equal 100 percent.

Figure 6–3
Relative contributions to profit.

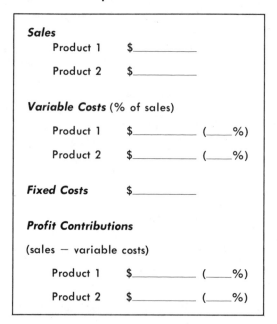

Sales

  Product 1 $_____

  Product 2 $_____

Variable Costs (% of sales)

  Product 1 $_____ (___%)

  Product 2 $_____ (___%)

Fixed Costs $_____

Profit Contributions

(sales − variable costs)

  Product 1 $_____ (___%)

  Product 2 $_____ (___%)

Enter the fixed costs for your two products and deduct them.

Assume administrative costs to be $100,000. Enter and deduct them. Operating profit is now the final amount to be determined.

Compare your answer with Figure 6-5. Note that the operating profit is $250,000. This is the amount of profit remaining after deducting $1,100,000 representing administrative and fixed costs. The amount of contribution to profits and fixed costs is $1,350,000. Of this total profit contribution, 44 percent is contributed by product 1 sales and 56 percent is contributed by product 2 sales.

Of total sales for the period of $3,500,000, 57 percent represents product 1 sales and 43 percent represents product 2 sales. Product 2 sales contribute a relatively greater portion of the profit contribution than the proportion of its sales to total sales.

Figure 6–4
Operating statement.

	TOTAL	PRODUCT 1	PRODUCT 2
Sales	$	$	$
Percent of total	100%	%	%
Variable Costs	$	$	$
Percent of sales	%	%	%
Contribution to Profit	$	$	$
Percent of total	100%	%	%
Fixed Costs	$		
Administrative Expense	$100,000		
Operating Profit			
Percent of sales	%		

RELATE CONTRIBUTION MARGIN
TO YOUR OWN PRODUCT LINE

Now that you have practiced figuring the contribution margin of the products in the case history, use the same approach for your own product line. First, work up the fact base for each of your key products or services by itemizing *sales* (amount and percent), *variable costs*, *contribution*, and *fixed costs*.

Then use Figure 6-1 as a model to visualize for each product or service its sales figure at the bottom of each of

Figure 6–5
Operating statement.

	TOTAL	PRODUCT 1	PRODUCT 2
Sales	$3,500,000	$2,000,000	$1,500,000
Percent of total	100%	57%	43%
Variable Costs	$2,150,000	$1,400,000	$ 750,000
Percent of sales	61%	70%	50%
Product Percent			
Contribution		30%	50%
Contribution to Profit	$1,350,000	$ 600,000	$ 750,000
Percent of total	100%	44%	56%
Fixed Costs	$1,000,000		
Administrative Expense	$ 100,000		
Operating Profit	$ 250,000		
Percent of sales	7%		

the upper set of bar graphs. Calculate the variable costs for each product. Scale off on the upper bar graph the sales amounts for each product. The remaining segment of each bar graph represents each product's contribution margin.

Next, enter the amount and percentage of each product's contribution margin. In the lower set of bar graphs, scale off the amount of each product's contribution margin and enter the amount at the bottom of each lower bar graph. Scale off the amount of fixed costs and enter the amount where it is indicated. The remaining segment of the contribution margin represents each product's operating profit.

Now that you know each individual product's contribution margin, use Figure 6-3 as a model to compare each product's relative annual contribution.

Figure 6-4 is a simplified operating statement. Use it as a model to enter the numbers you have worked up for each of your key products or services along with their totals. Round all numbers to whole numbers. Make the total possible contribution from all your products equal to 100 percent. When you have calculated the individual contributions of each key product or service, their sum should therefore be 100 percent.

Now that you know the profit contribution which each product or service makes to your line, you will be able to allocate your best salespeople and your largest budgets to pushing the big winners. You may end up by applying as much as 80 percent of your effort against only 20 percent or so of your products because they are the major profit makers for you. Every dollar you spend elsewhere may earn less for you and may also deprive you of the chance to maximize the return on its investment by using it to support a big winner.

III
How
to
plan
your
territory
sales
growth

7

How to target your heavy-user customers

Your territory, like all territories, is made up of two kinds of customers. There is a small number of heavy users of your products and services, customers who use them in large volume on a repetitive basis and who reorder loyally with the greatest frequency. These heavy users may constitute 20 percent or less of your total customers. The second kind of customer is the light or periodic user. This group may constitute 80 percent or more of your total customers.

This heavy user/light user breakout is the basis of the universal 80-20 rule that says as much as 80 percent of your profitable sales volume can come from as few as 20 percent of your customers. They are the key account group you must plan for. If you can zero in on their needs and offer them the product or service values they perceive to be the most beneficial, you can improve your penetration of the most profitable market available to you.

Your heavy-user customers must determine two aspects of your sales growth planning: (1) your *sales growth objectives*, which will be largely dependent on the penetration you can make into heavy-user demand; and (2) your *sales growth strategies*, which must offer the highest value-to-price benefits to your heavy users.

In Figure 7-1 enter the names of your heaviest users in descending rank order of use. Opposite each name put down your plan for the heavy-user account's contribution to this year's profit and sales objectives. Then also put down the account's projected next year's contributions. If you do not know profit contributions, estimate them. Your heavy-user contributions should be about 80 percent of your total objectives.

If next year's projections for a heavy-user customer promise higher profit, you have a good profit grower. If next year's projections are lower, you are in danger of having a heavy user pass into light-user status. Take remedial action at once, either to boost his contribution back to heavy-user status or to replace his contribution by developing other heavy-user customers.

HEAVY-USER NEEDS AUDIT

Use Figure 7-2 to copy the names of your heavy-user product customers as you set them down in Figure 7-1. Opposite each name, list the customer's major needs. These needs will almost always be for some form of profit improvement: either new sales revenues or reduced costs. Sometimes other needs must also be met. This will give you an idea of the customer opportunities for you to target on in order to grow your business. By focusing on your heavy-user needs, you will be able to answer important management questions such as these: Are we concentrating on serving our heavy users' needs? Are my salespeople wasting time calling on

Figure 7-1
Heavy-user customer contribution plan.

	PLANNED CONTRIBUTION TO THIS YEAR'S OBJECTIVES		PROJECTED CONTRIBUTION TO NEXT YEAR'S OBJECTIVES	
HEAVY-USER CUSTOMERS	PROFIT	SALES	PROFIT	SALES

Figure 7-2
Heavy-user customer needs audit.

	MAJOR NEEDS		
HEAVY-USER CUSTOMERS	FOR NEW SALES REVENUES	FOR REDUCED COSTS	OTHER

marginal customers? How do we define a marginal customer so that we know the minimum profit contribution and sales volume where heaviness of use begins?

Figure 7-3 shows an in-depth method of analyzing a key customer account. Among the chief benefits of such a record are that major revenue producers can be even more intensively sold to; key account knowledge survives salesman turnover;

81

Figure 7–3
Key account analysis.

Figure 7–3. Key account analysis.

Name _____
Address _____
City _____ State _____
Telephone _____ / _____

Type of business and market segments served

	Name	Title	Key Traits and Characteristics
Key buying influences (in rank order of importance)	1.		
	2.		
	3.		
Customer needs from us (in rank order of importance)	4.		7.
	5.		8.
	6.		9.
Our products and services used (in rank order of sales volume)	1.		4. 7.
	2.		5. 8.
	3.		6. 9.

Sales ($000)	19 __ __ Obj.	Actual	19 __ __ Obj.	Actual	19 __ __ Obj.	Actual	19 __ __ Obj.	Actual
Products								
Equipment and supplies								
Systems								
Services								

Competitors (in rank order of importance)

Company name	Competitive strengths	Competitive weaknesses
1.		
2.		
3.		

Growth opportunity analysis

Opportunities and obstacles to growth

and new salesmen can catch on quickly to key customer needs. What is more, the record helps to orient all staff personnel to heavy-user needs and acts as a reference when planning must be done.

HEAVY-USER SALES TERRITORY ORGANIZATION

As part of your concentration on heavy-user customers, you should organize the development of your sales territory to make the best resolution of four factors: (1) types of key accounts to be developed, (2) number of key accounts of each type, (3) profit value and gross sales volume value of each key account, and (4) cumulative call time required to develop the full profit value of each key account.

To develop heavy-user customer potential to the fullest, the most important criterion to follow with your salesforce is not the number of calls per month but the *cumulative call time* invested monthly or quarterly. Every key account requires intensive development. The sheer number of calls made on such an account is an imperfect index of development. What matters most is the amount of time intensively applied by each sales representative in actively penetrating an account—that is, in selling to its decision makers and their influencers with the depth and consistency required in order to be converted and maintained as a customer that uses your products and services heavily.

Cumulative call-time bogeys should be established on the basis of your estimate of each account's actual or potential profitability, not just its sales volume. Every key account should have a minimum CCT bogey assigned to it. This will represent your estimate of the smallest amount of time required to produce the targeted profit on sales. Every key account should also have a maximum CCT bogey. This will represent the greatest amount of time you are willing to see invested by each sales representative in developing the account's budgeted profitable sales volume. Use Figure 7–4 as a model to set up a minimum and maximum cumulative call-time schedule for your heavy-user accounts.

Figure 7–4
Heavy-user account—cumulative call-time schedule.

	CUMULATIVE QUARTERLY CALL TIME			
	MINIMUM		MAXIMUM	
HEAVY-USER CUSTOMERS	HOURS / QUARTER	COST	HOURS / QUARTER	COST

KEY ACCOUNT CALL PLANNING

Every key account sales call is of prime importance. Business lost from a key account is the most damaging loss you can suffer. To avoid loss—and to make the sale—be sure that each of your salespeople uses a key account call plan. It will enable them to plan in advance of every call what they will say and do to support your overall objectives with the account. The key account call plan shown in Figure 7-5 has five major planning steps: (1) the salesman's objectives; (2) the account problems the salesman wants to solve; (3) the product or service benefits that will solve the problem; (4) the product or service features that will provide the benefits; and (5) the salesman's opening promise of profit improvement for the account, customer demands for justification which the salesman can anticipate, and his closing questions.

SELLING YOUR BIG WINNERS
TO YOUR HEAVY USERS

Just as the 80–20 rule applies to your customers, of whom about 20 percent are your heavy users, the same rule applies

Figure 7–5
Key account call plan.

Key account _____

Key decision makers to be called on:

_____

_____

---

1. Call objectives — accomplishments I want to come back with:

_____

_____

---

2. Situation survey Account's problems I want to solve	Benefits that will solve the problem (in rank order of importance)	Product/service features that will provide these benefits (in rank order of importance)
	1.	1.
	2.	2.
	3.	3.
	4.	4.
	5.	5.
	6.	6.

---

3. My opening promise of a profit improvement benefit:

_____

_____

_____

---

4. Demands for justification of my promise which I can anticipate:

1. _____

2. _____

3. _____

4. _____

---

5. My closing questions to insure that I have accomplished my
call objectives:

1. _____

2. _____

3. _____

to your product mix. As you have seen, about 20 percent of all the items in your product line can contribute as much as 80 percent of your profitable sales volume. These are your big winners. The ideal sales situation is to be able to sell your big winners to your heavy users.

In order to do this, you must know what your big winners are in terms of their contribution margin. Furthermore, you should know just how big each big winner is so that you can give your salesforce a priority rank order for the sale of your biggest profit makers.

Contribution margin will tell you what your big winners are contributing at any given moment in their life cycle. It can also tell you what their contribution trend has been like over the past few years. You can project these trends and get a rough idea of the future. It will help you get a better fix on the future contribution you can expect from each product if you plot its position on a life cycle curve that will reflect its profitability. Not only will you have a graphic representation of its contribution. You will also be able to preview the opportunities you may have for extending its profit run or restoring it.

When a product is relatively new in its market, or enjoys exclusivity, it holds brand status. This means it can usually command a premium price and return a premium profit. Its major sales growth is still ahead of it. On the other hand, products that have been on the market for a long time and no longer enjoy exclusivity, or are not perceived by their customers to be worth a premium price, must usually be sold at commodity prices. Their profit margins will probably be small even though their sales volume may be large.

Since growth profits are made in "brand country," profit making means always having a sufficient number of big-winner brands in your strategy mix.

Profit pattern analysis is a method for determining whether you are adequately represented with big-winner products that are in the growth phases of their life cycles. Figure 7-6 shows an ideal profit pattern curve. The curve's horizontal base represents time. It shows how many years a product has been on the market. The curve's vertical axis represents sales volume. It shows how many gross sales dollars the product

Figure 7–6
Ideal profit pattern.

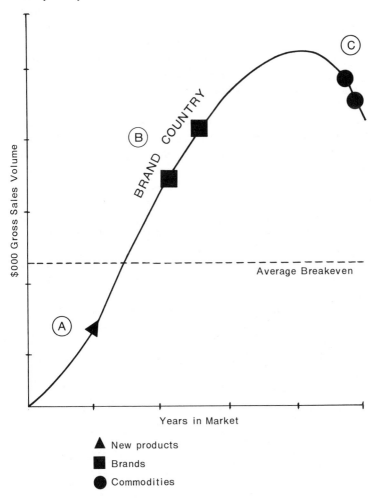

▲ New products

■ Brands

● Commodities

is contributing. By locating the point on the profit pattern where years and dollars intersect, it is possible to tell how many sales dollars a product is grossing at its current phase of life and to estimate its profit contribution.

In the model, a new product is represented by a triangle in phase A of its profit pattern. Its sales are below breakeven.

It is not yet a big winner since it is not earning any profit even though sales may be high. In phase B, two squares represent established products which are generating profitable sales volume in the curve's "brand country." Their profits are ahead of their sales. Some of them may become big winners. In phase C, the two circles represent commodity products. They have been big winners. Depending on their profit contribution, they may still be.

This profit pattern curve is called an ideal because it shows a business that appears to be in good shape. Its branded products in the phase B area yield a high rate of profitable sales volume. If all products were concentrated in phase A or phase C, the profit outlook would be far less positive. This is true for two reasons.

First, new products add more to costs than profits. If they become successful, their profit on sales improves in proportion to the number of years they have been on the market. Then it levels off.

Second, older products can still add importantly to profits but their profit per unit is generally on a progressive decline.

Use Figure 7-6 to identify your big winners that generate your premium profits. Fill in the proper numbers on the vertical sales axis and the horizontal time axis. Draw an average breakeven line above which profits are made. Then, using the curve as a rough guideline, locate the approximate position of your big winner products.

Use triangles to represent new products, squares to represent your big winner brands, and circles to represent your commodity products. Then, on Figure 7-7, put down the planned contribution to this year's and next year's objectives of each big winner product you have identified.

BIG WINNER/HEAVY USER MATCH-UP

To grow a new product into a big winner, and then to maintain it as a premium profit brand, your product must be matched to offer the best solution to your heavy users' major needs. The best solution is usually the one that promises a heavy user the greatest profit improvement in the operation

Figure 7–7
Big winner product audit.

	PLANNED CONTRIBUTION TO THIS YEAR'S OBJECTIVES		PROJECTED CONTRIBUTION TO NEXT YEAR'S OBJECTIVES	
BIG WINNER PRODUCTS	PROFIT	SALES	PROFIT	SALES

Figure 7–8
Big winner/heavy user product match-up.

	MAJOR NEEDS			
HEAVY-USER CUSTOMERS	FOR NEW SALES REVENUES	FOR REDUCED COSTS	BIG WINNER PRODUCTS	BIG WINNER BENEFITS TO MEET HEAVY-USER NEEDS

of one or more of his major functions, operations, or processes. This is the solution for which heavy users are willing to pay a premium price because solutions that deliver profit improvement command the highest value-to-price relationship. This, in turn, helps insure your own premium profit on sales.

Use Figure 7-8 to enter the names of your heavy-user customers and their major needs as you set them down in

Figure 7-2. Then, opposite each need, list your big winner products and their benefits that can promise the highest value-to-price solution for your customer and you.

8
How to forecast your sales

Newly appointed managers often find forecasting to be one of the most difficult aspects of sales management. They realize its crucial importance: Virtually every major function in their companies is geared to the sales forecast. But because forecasting deals with the future, they make a guessing game of it. Some managers make forecasting a form of management roulette. A few play it safe, underestimating on the conservative side to make their eventual performance look better than it actually is. Strangely enough, most of these diversions require more effort and anxiety than following a forecasting planning schedule that yields an accurate, defensible estimate of sales and profit.

To simplify your forecasting responsibilities, use the forecasting planning schedule in Figure 8-1 as a guideline. Follow it step by step. Start by choosing one of your big winner products to forecast. Enter its name on the planning schedule. Then repeat the schedule's forecasting process for each big winner. In this way you will be able to forecast the major share, perhaps up to 80 percent, of your annual sales and profit. You can then either repeat the schedule for your remaining products or simply estimate their contribution at around 20 percent of your total annual sales and profits.

Figure 8–1
Forecast planning schedule.

PRODUCT: _____

1. *Sales Objectives*
   1.1. This year gross profit on
      product sales   = $ ___,___,___
         As a result of:
   1.2. This year total product sales
      volume   =   #___,___,___
   1.3. This year total product sales
      volume   = $ ___,___,___

2. *Last Year / Year Before Rate of*
   Sales Growth   =   __%
   2.1. Unmodified forecast   =   #___,___,___

3. *Modified + / − This Year by:*
   3.1. Industry growth factor of
      + / − __%   = + / − #___,___,___
   3.2. Product life cycle growth
      factor of + / − __%   = + / − #___,___,___
   3.3. Business cycle growth factor
      of + / − __%   = + / − #___,___,___

4. *Modified + / − Further This Year*
   by:
   4.1. Competitive factor of + / −
      __%   = + / − #___,___,___

STEP 1: TARGET YOUR FORECAST
WITH YOUR SALES OBJECTIVES

Three types of sales objectives constitute the *must-get* targets of your sales growth plan. They are (1) gross profit on product sales, (2) unit sales volume, (3) dollar sales volume. Take the first step in making your forecast by entering your three must-get targets in items 1.1, 1.2, and 1.3 on Figure 8–1.

Figure 8–1 (continued)

4.2. Market need factor of $+/-$
 __% $= +/- $ #___,___,___

4.3. Legislative factor of $+/-$
 __% $= +/- $ #___,___,___

4.4. Technology factor of $+/-$
 __% $= +/- $ #___,___,___

4.5. Energy and materials factor
 of $+/-$ __% $= +/- $ #___,___,___

5. *Sum of All Modifications* $= +/- $ #___,___,___
 Add to or subtract from
 unmodified forecast (item 2) to
 determine modified forecast.
 Enter modified forecast in item
 6.1.1.

6. *Sales Forecast*
 6.1. *Product Sales for Forecast
 Period*
    6.1.1. Sales in units $\times$
       price/unit = \$___ $=$ #___,___,___

    6.1.2. Sales in dollars $=$ \$ ___,___,___
 6.2. *Product Sales Per Month*
    6.2.1. Average sales in
       units/month $=$ #___,___,___
    6.2.2. Average sales in
       dollars/month $=$ \$ ___,___,___
 6.3. *Gross Profit on Product Sales* $=$ \$ ___,___,___
 6.4. *Average Gross Profit on
 Sales/Month* $=$ \$ ___,___,___

STEP 2: MAKE AN UNMODIFIED
FORECAST OF PRODUCT UNIT SALES

If the rate of *last year's sales growth over the year before* were to continue without modification, what would your rate of sales growth be for *this year?* Figure it out this way:

$$\frac{\text{Sales}}{\text{Last Year}} \times \frac{\text{Sales the}}{\text{Year Before}} = \left\{ \begin{array}{l} +/-\text{ \% Rate} \\ \text{of Growth} \end{array} \right.$$

Total industry
Unit sales = #__,___,___ × $__,___,___ = ___%
Dollar sales = $__,___,___ × $__,___,___ = ___%
Our product
Unit sales = #__,___,___ × $__,___,___ = ___%
Dollar sales = $__,___,___ × $__,___,___ = ___%

Take the second step in making your forecast by entering your last year/year before rate of sales growth in item 2 of Figure 8-1. Then enter your unmodified unit sales volume forecast in item 2.1. Is your rate of growth better than the industry rate? Worse? The same? You must grow sales faster than the industry rate in order to have a growth product and a growth business. Is your share of market growing? Shrinking? Static? Increased profit often depends directly on increased market share, especially in the growth stage of product life. Figure your share of market according to the following formula:

$$\frac{\text{Our product unit sales last year}}{\text{Total industry unit sales last year}} = \text{\% market share}$$

STEP 3: MODIFY CURRENT RATE OF SALES GROWTH
BY THIS YEAR'S STAGE OF THREE CYCLES

There are three cycles which can affect your current rate of product sales growth. They are your industry growth cycle, your product life cycle, and the business cycle.

Cycle 1—your industry's stage in its growth cycle. If your industry grew last year, will it continue to grow at the same rate this year? In other words, is the industry's growth cycle likely to remain at the same stage? If it is, you can assume that your sales will also grow at the same rate. If not, you will have to modify your sales growth up or down. Enter your modification in percentage and unit volume terms in item 3.1 of Figure 8-1.

Cycle 2—your product's stage in its life cycle. If your product sales grew last year, will they continue to grow at the same rate this year? In other words, is your product likely to remain at the same stage in its life cycle? If it is, you can assume your sales will also grow at the same rate. If your product is moving up the growth slope of its life cycle curve, you can assume that your sales will grow at a faster rate. If your product is moving down the slope of the curve, you can assume that your sales will grow at a slower rate or that they may even decline. Enter your modification in percentage and unit volume terms in item 3.2 of Figure 8-1. Keep in mind that your product's stage in its growth cycle plays a significant role in determining price and promotional investment.

Price. Premium price can be most easily charged in a life cycle's growth and early maturity stages. Premium prices boost dollar sales volume.

Promotional investment. Promotion is generally heaviest in a life cycle's growth and early maturity stages. It will usually decrease and may even cease in maturity and decline.

In order to position your product in its life cycle, use Figure 8-2 to divide the years-of-commercial-life axis into the number of years that accurately reflect your product's total commercial life. Divide the vertical axis into units of the product's sales volume. Write the letters LY (last year) on the curve where your product's commercial life and last year's sales volume intersect. Write the letters YB (year before) on the curve where your product's commercial life and year before sales volume intersect. This shows whether sales are growing or declining. If sales are moving up, your product may still be in the growth stage of its life cycle. If sales appear to be moving down, your product may be mature or in decline.

Cycle 3—the economy's stage in the business cycle. If the economy grew last year, will it continue to grow at the

Figure 8–2
Product life cycle.

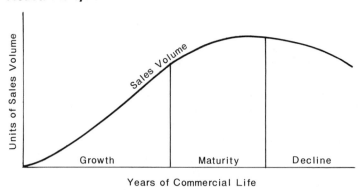

same rate this year? If the answer is yes, you can assume that your sales will also grow at the same rate. If not, you will have to modify your sales growth up or down. Enter your modification in percentage and unit volume terms in item 3.3 of Figure 8.1.

STEP 4: MODIFY CURRENT RATE OF SALES GROWTH BY THE PROBABLE EFFECTS OF FIVE UNKNOWABLE FACTORS

There are five influential factors whose effects you cannot ever fully know beforehand. Whenever you assume they will change, you will also have to change your assumptions about the rate of positive or negative sales growth to expect. The five factors are competition, market needs, legislation, technology, and the availability of energy and materials.

Factor 1—your major competitors' probable intentions. What do you assume your major competitors intend to do this year that can increase or decrease your sales? If your competitors are most likely to do nothing different from last year, you can assume your sales will grow at the same rate as far as competitive activity is concerned. If not, you will have to modify your sales growth up or down. Enter your modification in percentage and unit volume terms in item 4.1 of Figure 8-1.

Keep in mind that competition can come from three sources: established competitors, new competitors, and indirect competitors who market substitute products. Competition from any of these sources can play a significant role in determining your price. Competition can also telescope your product's life cycle and accelerate its entry into maturity and decline, putting a brake on your profitable sales growth.

Factor 2—your market's probable needs. What do you assume your market's needs will be this year? If they will probably be the same as last year, you can assume that your sales will grow at the same rate as far as market demand is concerned. If not, you will have to modify your sales growth up or down. Enter your modification in percentage and unit volume terms in item 4.2 of Figure 8-1.

Factor 3—the probable effects of legislation. What laws do you assume will be passed by government agencies at the local, state, or federal level that can increase or decrease your sales? If no legislation is likely, you can assume that your sales will grow at the same rate as far as legal constraints are concerned. If not, you will have to modify your sales growth up or down. Enter your modification in percentage and unit volume terms in item 4.3 of Figure 8-1.

Factor 4—the probable effects of technology. What technical or scientific innovations do you assume will be commercialized this year that can increase or decrease your sales? If no innovation is likely, you can assume that your sales will grow at the same rate as far as technical obsolescence is concerned. If not, you will have to modify your sales growth up or down. Enter your modification in percentage and unit volume terms in item 4.4 of Figure 8-1.

Factor 5—the probable effects of energy and materials availability. What energy or materials shortfalls do you assume can increase or decrease your sales? If no shortfalls are likely, you can assume that your sales will grow at the same rate as far as availabilities are concerned. If not, you will have to modify your sales growth up or down. Enter your modification in percentage and unit volume terms in item 4.5 of Figure 8-1.

Salesforce Contributions

You can forecast from the top down by imposing your forecast on your salesforce or you can forecast from the bottom up by allowing your salesforce to participate in the forecasting process. Whichever method you adopt, you will need salesforce information. There are three types of information which each salesperson in the field should contribute: (1) expectations of customer intentions, (2) expectations of competitive intentions, (3) expectations of effects of materials and energy availability on his own operations. Invite each of your salespeople to forecast his own sales of each product this year. Use Figure 8-3 as a model for this information. The sum of the sales representatives' forecasts must be made to equal your total sales forecast for the product.

Figure 8–3
Sales forecast.

PRODUCT (19__ to 19__) _____

Salesman _____

Region _____

YEAR AGO	ACTUAL SALES LAST YEAR	ACTUAL SALES THIS YEAR	FORECAST SALES*
#__,___,___	$ __,___,___	$ __,___,___	$ __,___,___
	#__,___,___	#__,___,___	

*This year forecast sales are based on the following expectations:

1. Customer intentions

2. Competitive intentions

3. Materials and energy availability

4. Other

Each sales representative's reward for his contribution of information is his *quota*. In assigning quotas to each, you should take into consideration five factors: (1) your overall annual sales objectives, which set the total profit and sales volume contributions you require for growth; (2) the mix of each sales representative's heavy-user customers and prospective customers in terms of their number, size, and location within his territory, and his estimated cumulative call-time schedule for them, which should allow for travel down time; (3) the sales representative's performance capability and productivity level as shown by experience, which should allow for the degree of competitive ferocity he encounters in his territory; (4) the sales representative's product mix, especially the number of big winners he has in his line; (5) the state of the economy in the sales representative's territory.

Every salesperson can be assigned a profit quota, a dollar sales volume quota, and an activity quota, in terms of required product demonstrations, applied services necessary to achieve sales, and other selling activities.

Improving your quota-making skill is a continuing job. You should be working at it all the time. To enable yourself to come progressively closer to quotas that reflect each sales representative's maximum contribution, follow these five suggestions:

1. Conduct monthly studies of actual sales compared against quotas on a salesman-by-salesman basis. Learn where you come closest and why.
2. Keep a record of past contributions on a salesman-by-salesman basis. Learn who the heavy producers and the poor producers are.
3. Keep current with changes in market potential on a salesman-by-salesman basis. Look for new businesses moving in or old businesses moving out, expanded or abandoned plants, increased or decreased competition, and so forth. Raise or lower your quotas accordingly.
4. Invite your salespeople to participate with you in suggesting their own quotas. Then invite them to

participate with you in their performance review on an actual vs. quota basis.

5. Ask your suppliers to share with you their own quotas for your territory. You may get valuable clues.

STEP 5: SUM UP ALL MODIFICATIONS

Sum up all the modifications of rate of sales growth that you have entered in items 3.1 through 4.5 on your *forecast planning schedule* in Figure 8-1. Enter this sum in unit volume terms in item 5. Apply it to item 2.1 to determine your modified forecast. Enter your *modified forecast* in item 6.1.1 of Figure 8-1.

STEP 6: MAKE YOUR SALES FORECAST

There are four key items of your *sales forecasts:* product sales for the forecast period, product sales per month, profit on your product sales, and profit per month.

FORECAST DOLLAR SALES AND PROFIT ON SALES

Up to now your forecast planning has concentrated on physical product unit volume. Now you must convert these units into dollars and, after that, you will have to translate dollars into profits.

Item 6.1.2—Convert unit sales into dollar sales. What is your forecast dollar sales volume? To convert units into dollars, use the following formula:

Product unit volume × price
            = product dollar volume $__,___,___

Enter your product dollar volume in item 6.1.2 of Figure 8-1.

Convert Dollar Sales into Profit

What is your forecast profit on sales? To convert dollars into profit at your product's gross margin level, use the following formula.

$$\frac{\text{Product dollar volume}}{\text{Product gross margin}} = \% \text{ profit}$$

If you do not know your product's gross margin, estimate it on the basis of your knowledge of similar products or on your assumptions as to whether the product is a big winner. Enter your gross dollar profit on product sales in item 6.3 of Figure 8-1.

FORECAST SALES AND PROFIT PER MONTH

As the final step, your forecast planning schedule calls for you to divide your forecast annual sales into average sales per month in terms of unit and dollar volume in items 6.2.1 and 6.2.2 of Figure 8-1. Then divide your forecast annual gross dollar profit on sales by 12 to ascertain your average monthly profit. Enter your average gross dollar profit on sales in item 6.4 of Figure 8-1. A monthly profit forecast is required for two main reasons. First, month-by-month profit forecasts confirm the ups and downs of a repetitive seasonal cycle and allow advertising, sales promotion, and direct selling to be concentrated cyclically or countercyclically. Second, month-by-month profit forecasts allow cash flow to be planned so that the ebb and flow of the stream of revenues into your business can be balanced against your expenditures.

9
How to set your sales growth objectives

To be a successful sales manager you must know the answers to two questions all the time. The first question is, Where is my business now? The second question is, Where am I taking my business? The answer to the first question will tell you what kind of business you are taking over: whether it is a growth business, a mature business, or a declining business. This will help you understand the base you have for growth. The answer to the second question will be your growth objectives.

If you are taking over a *new* business, your major tasks will be devoted to overcoming a lack of awareness of your product or service benefits and establishing initial distribution

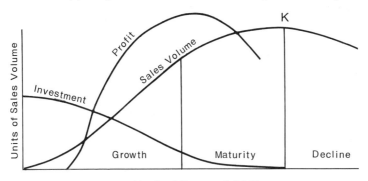

and market penetration. In this takeoff stage, demand must be accelerated and total market size expanded as rapidly as possible. Sales must grow and unit costs must be brought down so that unit profits can rise. If entry pricing has been set at a premium, your profits can be even further accelerated by creaming the market. To continue growth, you must expand the market among your heavy users. In addition, new heavy-user customers must be acquired. While distribution pipelines are being filled, the two most severe threats to your profit making are backordering or its opposite, inventory buildup.

You can tell if you are taking over a *mature* business by its relationship to point K in Figure 9-1. If it is near or beyond point K, premium price will be difficult for you to hold. Price competition will be intense and sales volume will generally level off as your competitors achieve market penetration based on marginal price or product differences. Your advertising and sales promotion expenditures will have to increase. Your cost of sales will rise because many of your original distribution outlets must be held by price and service concessions. More costs will be incurred as additional distribution must be sought out, educated, and supplied with products and motivation. While volume rises, profits may erode as price falls and deals or free services give away additional earnings opportunities. As maturity ripens, market growth will slow down to the replacement rate. This is the business half life, the halfway point in the commercial life of the business. This is the point where a technological or marketing advance may restore the business to greater profitability. If not, you must begin to restructure your business objectives to become a cash flow supplier for the funding of successor products or services.

If you are taking over a *declining* business, you will be managing a cost reduction operation in the face of increasing obsolescence and price competition. As your profit on sales declines, sales expenditures must also fall in order to shrink your cost base as much as possible. Growth becomes increasingly negative. Overcapacity may become evident and the number of competitive suppliers may recede. Product line smoothing will have to take place. So will other cost control measures. Profit can be maintained only by product or sales rejuvenation or by continued cost reduction.

THE BUSINESS VALUE
OF YOUR GROWTH OBJECTIVES

The profit-investment relationship over your business life cycle establishes two principles about making a profitable rate of return on investment.

First, profit accrues principally from new or rejuvenated products and services whose rate of return on investment is at its highest point. Therefore, the return on investment from your business will be composed chiefly of return on the investment of the big winner products and services that are in their growth phase.

Second, your profit objectives should be set in relation to the phase of your business in its life cycle. No business can be expected to earn a maximum rate of profit every year. Once profit reaches its maximum point, it must inevitably decline. Your annual profit objectives must therefore be oriented to the year's position in the business life cycle.

Objectives are sometimes referred to as goals, targets, or results. They are the reason you are in business. In a growing business, your objectives will be based on improving your position of a year ago. By improving your year-ago position, you add value to your territory. If your business starts to go bad, your objectives will be based on limiting your loss. Instead of adding to the value of your territory, you will have to be content to conserve as much of its existing value as possible. If you turn around a declining business you will be restoring value to your territory to the point where you can begin to add new value to it once again.

Objectives represent the value of your business. The best general answer to the question, Where am I taking my business? is, I am taking it to new values, represented by my growth objectives. There are three values that have to be added to your business to make it grow. One of the values is new profit. Another value is new gross sales dollars from which profits can be brought down. These sales dollars can be represented by the earnings from sales themselves or by the unit volume which produces them and the share of market they account for. The third value is a superior market position, or image, for your business.

Therefore, a more specific answer to the question, Where am I taking my business? is, I am taking it to new profits based on improved profit on unit sales which will help me strengthen my market position as the most preferred supplier.

THE SALES BASE
OF YOUR GROWTH OBJECTIVES

The purpose of setting sales objectives is to help you grow your business. Your existing business therefore becomes the base of your sales growth planning. Your objectives will be designed to add value to this base. This is the meaning of growth. Thus a sales manager can be defined as someone who adds value to his business base.

There are two attributes of your sales base that you must summarize in order to set objectives for the business growth you are planning to manage. First, make a summary of your present business base. Use Figure 9-2 to show you what you have to grow from. Along with the SIC number and name of each of your present key accounts, enter its location,

Figure 9–2
Present business base audit.

SIC INDUSTRY	NAME OF KEY ACCOUNT	LOCATION	LAST YEAR'S CONTRIBUTIONS		PERCENT OF TOTAL PRESENT BUSINESS REPRESENTED
			PROFIT ON SALES	SALES VOLUME	

the contributions it made last year to your profit on sales and dollar sales volume, and the percentage of your total present business the account represents. Then use Figure 9–3 to make a summary of your potential business growth opportu-

Figure 9–3
Potential business growth audit.

SIC INDUSTRY	NAME OF PROSPECTIVE ACCOUNT	LOCATION	EXPECTED NEXT YEAR'S CONTRIBUTION		PERCENT OF TOTAL GROWTH BUSINESS REPRESENTED
			PROFIT ON SALES	SALES VOLUME	

nity. Enter the name of each prospective account, its location, the contribution you expect it to make next year to your profit on sales and dollar sales volume, and the percentage of your total growth business the account could represent.

THE THREE KINDS OF OBJECTIVES

There are three kinds of objectives that can add value to your sales growth. The first is *financial*. These objectives are the numbers that tell you how profitably you are managing your business. For this reason, financial objectives are primary objectives. The second kind are *sales objectives*, which underlie financial objectives. Sales objectives make financial objectives possible and for this reason, can be regarded as contributory objectives. Another contributory objective is the *market position objective*, which underlies sales objectives.

Figure 9-4 shows this hierarchy of objectives. First, you must determine the financial objectives you want to achieve. Second, you must figure out the sales objectives you will need in order to achieve your financial objectives. Third, you must decide the best market positioning for your business that will help you achieve your sales objectives.

Figure 9–4
Hierarchy of objectives.

Primary Objectives
   1. *Financial Objectives*
      1.1. Profit on sales
      1.2. Return on investment
Contributory Objectives
   2. *Sales Objectives*
      2.1. Dollar sales volume
      2.2. Unit sales volume
      2.3. Share of market penetration
   3. *Market Position Objectives*

1. FINANCIAL OBJECTIVES

As a sales manager, you must make profit the name of your game. Profit is the number of dollars which remain from dollar sales volume after the cost of attaining that sales volume has been subtracted. Sales volume in itself is not an adequate standard of performance because it is perfectly possible to have a high dollar sales volume but a low or nonexistent profit, and it is also possible to have a relatively high profit on a small dollar sales volume. *Profit on sales* must therefore be one of your two major financial objectives.

Profit is expressed in dollars. The second of your two financial objectives must be set as a percentage. This percentage compares your profit to the investment you are making to achieve it. This comparative ratio between profit and investment is your rate of *return on investment*, or ROI for short.

The basic ROI formula defines profit as the rate of profit on sales or, to say the same thing in another way, operating profit as a percentage of sales. Investment is defined as the total capital assets employed to produce your sales. Return on investment compares profit margin with asset turnover— that is, your earnings in terms of gross sales income and the capital assets employed to generate them. These relationships are shown in Figure 9–5. Because it accounts so comprehensively for the major activities of a business, ROI is generally

Figure 9–5
Return on investment formula.

$$\text{ROI} = \underset{\textit{as Return on Sales}}{\underbrace{\frac{\text{net operating profit expressed as income from earnings}}{\text{sales}}}} \times \underset{\textit{as Capital Turnover}}{\underbrace{\frac{\text{sales}}{\text{total investment in capital assets employed}}}}$$

Profit Margin Expressed as Return on Sales   *Return on Capital Expressed as Capital Turnover*

$$\frac{\text{Profit}}{\text{Investment}} = \text{earnings as a \% of sales} \times \text{asset turnover}$$

the best way of expressing the yield on total capital employed, both human and nonhuman. ROI can be *determined* by comparing predicted profit against investment. But in order to understand how ROI can be *managed,* you have to examine separately two attributes of return on investment: turnover and operating profit.

Turnover improvement. Figure 9-6 shows the three options that you can affect to improve turnover: inventories, receivables, and sales. By reducing the amount of funds invested in inventories, for example, you can help reduce the total investment base of your business. As a result, you can improve your planned profit objective by reducing cost.

Use Figure 9-6 to create a turnover improvement strategy that will help you improve your profit objective.

Operating profit improvement. Figure 9-7 shows the four options that you can affect to improve operating profit: cost of sales, selling expense, your share of administrative expense, and sales. By reducing the cost of sales, for example, you can help reduce the total cost structure of your business. As a result, you can improve your planned profit objective by reducing cost.

Use Figure 9-7 to create an operating profit improvement strategy that will help you improve your profit objective.

Figure 9–6
Turnover improvement strategy.

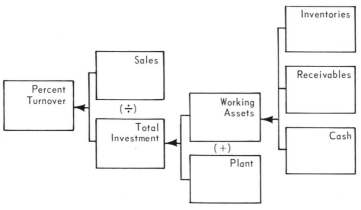

Figure 9–7
Operating profit improvement strategy.

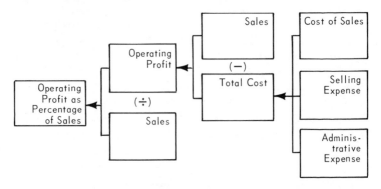

Your two financial objectives can be summarized in this way: (1) You must try to preserve as many dollars as possible from your dollar sales volume. The dollars you save will become your profit on sales. (2) You must try to keep your investment base as low as possible in relation to your profit on sales. This will help you achieve a high rate of return on investment.

Use Figure 9–8 to set down rough profit on sales figures

Figure 9–8
Annual profit on sales audit.

	DOLLAR SALES VOLUME		COST OF ACHIEVING DOLLAR SALES VOLUME		PROFIT ON SALES
Last year (19__)	$__,___,___	(−)	$__,___,___	=	$__,___,___
Budgeted for this year (19__)	$__,___,___	(−)	$__,___,___	=	$__,___,___
Estimated for next year (19__)	$__,___,___	(−)	$__,___,___	=	$__,___,___

Figure 9–9
Annual return on investment audit.

	PROFIT		INVESTMENT		RETURN ON INVESTMENT
Last year (19__)	$__,___,___	(÷)	$__,___,___	=	__%
Budgeted for this year (19__)	$__,___,___	(÷)	$__,___,___	=	__%
Estimated for next year (19__)	$__,___,___	(÷)	$__,___,___	=	__%

for last year, this year, and next year. Then transfer to the profit column of Figure 9-9 the figures you have entered for profit. Also transfer your figures on the cost of achieving your dollar sales volume and enter them in the investment column. Use these figures to calculate an approximate rate of return for your business for this year and next year, as well as what it was last year.

Avoiding the Sales Volume Trap

Increased sales volume can be a shortsighted objective. The belief that increased sales volume contributes automatically to increased profits—and therefore that it increases return on investment—is often a fiction. Profits do not always improve with sales volume. Even if profits do improve, their rate of improvement may be so low that increased sales are being purchased unprofitably.

What is really important is not so much the profit on sales but the *rate of profit on sales.* Unless the rate is maintained or increased as sales expand, increased sales volume may contribute nothing to maintain or increase your return on investment. In fact, if increased sales volume entails additional investment costs or reduced income due to lower prices, your return on investment will be reduced instead of increased.

There is always pressure for sales growth. If your business is not operating at capacity, the pressure will be phrased in the interest of utilizing underemployed assets. If your business is operating at capacity or close to it, the pressure will be phrased in the interest of taking advantage of existing sales momentum. Both kinds of pressure generate their own added costs which may, in the end, nullify whatever additional sales volume is achieved.

Acknowledging Uncertainty

The process of planning sales objectives is a risky undertaking because the future—the time frame being planned for—is always uncertain. It is therefore wise to build an acknowledgment of uncertainty into your planning so that the unexpected can become more expected. The best way to do this is to make three projections of objectives for each year you plan for:

1. A *best case* objective that you believe can be achieved if everything works out as planned.
2. An *average case* objective that you believe can be achieved if most things work out as planned or at least if the most important things work out.
3. A *worst case* objective that you believe can be achieved even if most things do not work out as planned.

The numerical difference between best and average cases and between average and worst cases should be no more than about 10 percent. This means that your best case objective will be a maximum of two times or so higher than the worst case. No sales plan should ever be put into effect if only the best case is acceptable. Nor should any plan ever be put into effect unless the business could survive if the worst case came true.

Use Figure 9-10 to work out best case, average case, and worst case objectives for this year. Check your results with the numbers you have been using in Figures 9-8 and 9-9. If you find that you have unwittingly been using best case figures, do two things. First, correct them to more average figures. Second, guard against being overoptimistic in your

Figure 9–10
Best/worst case analysis.

KEY INDICATORS FOR THIS YEAR	BEST CASE	AVERAGE CASE	WORST CASE
1. Financial Objectives			
1.1. *Profit on Sales*	$__,___,___	$__,___,___	$__,___,___
1.2. *Return on Investment*	__%	__%	__%
2. Sales Objectives			
2.1. *Dollar Sales Volume*	$__,___,___	$__,___,___	$__,___,___
2.1.1. Products	__,___,___	__,___,___	__,___,___
2.1.2. Services	__,___,___	__,___,___	__,___,___
2.2. *Unit Sales Volume*	$__,___,___	$__,___,___	$__,___,___
2.2.1. Products	__,___,___	__,___,___	__,___,___
2.2.2. Services	__,___,___	__,___,___	__,___,___
2.3. *Share of Market Penetration*	__%	__%	__%
2.3.1. Products	__	__	__
2.3.2. Services	__	__	__

113

future planning. On the other hand, you may unwittingly have been using worst case figures. When you correct them to more average figures, remind yourself to guard against being overpessimistic in your future planning.

2. SALES OBJECTIVES

Sales objectives are your second kind of objectives. Sales objectives support financial objectives by contributing to profit and return on investment. The three major sales objectives of dollar sales volume, unit sales volume, and percentage share of market penetration correlate directly with one another in some ways. In other ways they may correlate inversely. For example, dollar and unit sales volume do not always go together. A high dollar sales volume can be achieved at relatively low unit volume if high-priced units are being pushed

Figure 9–11
Sales contribution to profit audit.

	PROFIT ON SALES	SOURCES OF CONTRIBUTION TO PROFIT		
Last year (19__)	$__,___,___	$ Sales volume	=	$__,___,___
		# Sales volume	=	__,___,___
		% Share of market	=	__%
Budgeted for this year (19__)	$__,___,___	$ Sales volume	=	$__,___,___
		# Sales volume	=	__,___,___
		% Share of market	=	__%
Estimated for next year (19__)	$__,___,___	$ Sales volume	=	$__,___,___
		# Sales volume	=	__,___,___
		% Share of market	=	__%

over lower-priced units. A high percentage share of market generally accompanies a high unit sales volume. But high market share is not necessarily associated with high dollar sales volume. Furthermore, none of the three sales objectives is directly tied to profit. It is perfectly possible to have a high dollar and unit sales volume along with a high percentage share of market without earning a correspondingly high profit. As a matter of fact, one of the surest ways for a business to go broke is to stress high volume and pay no attention to whether the volume is profitable. If the investment base required to achieve it exceeds income, high volume cannot be profitable.

Use Figure 9-11 to correlate the contribution which each of your three sales objectives can make to achieving your profit objective. Calculate the average case dollar sales volume, unit sales volume, and percentage share of market required to achieve your planned profit on sales for this year and next year, as well as what it was last year. Use Figure 9-12 to break out your sales contribution to profit for this year on a quarter-by-quarter basis.

3. MARKET POSITION OBJECTIVE

When you have planned your financial objectives and the sales objectives that will contribute to them, you will then have to plan to achieve the market position you require in order to support these objectives.

Your market position is the image your business must enjoy in the minds of your key customer accounts if you are to achieve your sales and financial objectives. A literal definition of *market position* is how your business stands in key customer attitudes: how it is competitively known and what aspects of superiority it is known for. Your market position therefore becomes your customers' definition of your business.

To position your business properly, you must customer-target its definition. This means that you must make your business known as the preferred supplier of the most meaning-ful benefits that will meet your key accounts' major needs.

Figure 9–12
Quarterly/monthly sales contribution to profit audit.

MONTH	PROFIT ON SALES	$ SALES VOLUME	# SALES VOLUME
January	$ ---,---,---	$ ---,---,---	---,---,---
February	$ ---,---,---	$ ---,---,---	---,---,---
March	$ ---,---,---	$ ---,---,---	---,---,---
Quarter 1 totals	$ ---,---,---	$ ---,---,---	---,---,---
April	$ ---,---,---	$ ---,---,---	---,---,---
May	$ ---,---,---	$ ---,---,---	---,---,---
June	$ ---,---,---	$ ---,---,---	---,---,---
Quarter 2 totals	$ ---,---,---	$ ---,---,---	---,---,---
July	$ ---,---,---	$ ---,---,---	---,---,---
August	$ ---,---,---	$ ---,---,---	---,---,---
September	$ ---,---,---	$ ---,---,---	---,---,---
Quarter 3 totals	$ ---,---,---	$ ---,---,---	---,---,---
October	$ ---,---,---	$ ---,---,---	---,---,---
November	$ ---,---,---	$ ---,---,---	---,---,---
December	$ ---,---,---	$ ---,---,---	---,---,---
Quarter 4 totals	$ ---,---,---	$ ---,---,---	---,---,---
Annual totals	$ ---,---,---	$ ---,---,---	---,---,---

Figure 9–13
Market position statement.

My Business Will Be Positioned As:

1. A supplier of the profit improvement benefits of (cost reduction or increased new revenues or both)

2. To (the type of key account customers you have elected to serve)

3. By solving their major problems of (identify nature of problems and the customer processes they affect)

4. With (the major strategies you will apply).

These benefits must ultimately provide improved profitability for your customers. You can accomplish this by helping your customers reduce the costs of one or more of their major operations or processes. Or you may contribute improvements to their processes that will enable them to earn increased revenues from sales. In both cases, you will be contributing to their profit improvement by helping them solve a principal problem.

Use Figure 9-13 as a model to write out a statement in the traditional 25 words or so that will set forth the market position you want to achieve for your business. This statement will become the foundation for your repute as a supplier. Note that the market position statement requires four decisions: the kind of profit improvement benefits you will supply, the kind of key account customers to whom you will supply these benefits, the customer problems they solve, and the major product and service strategies you will apply to these problems in order to solve them.

IV
How
to
develop
your
salesforce

10
How to teach customer need analysis

Teaching your salespeople how to map the personalities of their customer decision makers can help them predict the buying actions their customers are most likely to take in competitive situations. It will also enable your salespeople to influence customer action in their favor.

In order to achieve a high degree of advance understanding of their customers' most probable buying behavior, you will have to teach your salespeople how to use their perceptions to map four aspects of customer personality: (1) cognitive style, (2) conative tendencies, (3) social and emotional characteristics, and (4) attitudes.

TEACH THE PRINCIPLES
OF PERCEPTIVE PROFILING

In your salespeople's day-to-day negotiation with their customers, they require only the use of their trained eyes and ears to perceive their customers' personalities. There are five principles of perception for them to follow in constructing a profile of each decision maker's style, tendencies, and characteristics.

1. *Observe.* Observation is the simplest principle of perception to teach your salespeople to put into practice. All they have to do is watch and listen. Yet they must carry on their watching and listening with empathy. Observation requires concentrated, disciplined attention to the cues and signals sent out by customers. The major problem that must be overcome is failing to see clearly what is really out there and, instead, perceiving only what they need or want to see. Their own selective inattention is potentially their worst enemy. It can lead them to make self-fulfilling prophecies by allowing them to see only what they look for and then encouraging them to use it to substantiate their original expectations.

2. *Get around.* Because your sales representatives must penetrate deeply and widely throughout their customer organizations, they must become masters of the art of crossing organizational lines without making the organization's leaders cross. Only by getting around can they hope to identify the key power figures who influence or determine the decision-making process. Beyond knowing who the decision makers are, your salespeople must in turn make themselves known as problem solvers who can help improve the organization's profit.

3. *Make alliances.* As they broadcast their offer of improved profit throughout the influential areas of their customers' organizations, your salespeople will be acting as advertisers for themselves. Their customer organizations are their media. Like all advertisers, they must acquire testimonials in their favor. Their testifiers can then become their internal sponsors. They must therefore be taught to make alliances with key influencers in their accounts. They must be careful to choose them not just by title or function but by their ability

to exert influence on the sellers' behalf. If your salespeople select their influencers well and learn their frames of reference, the influencers can act as extra pairs of eyes and ears which will multiply each salesperson's access throughout the customer organizations.

4. *Understand, don't judge.* A sales representative who allows himself to become emotionally involved with his customers so that he begins to feel sympathetically in favor of or against them, instead of feeling empathically with them, will find himself playing judge. He will choose sides, moralize, be opinionated. As soon as this happens, his objectivity is gone. Along with it goes his chance to make accurate perceptions. You must therefore teach your salespeople to restrict their involvement to the level at which understanding takes place, not judgment. They will always have their own preferences and prejudices about customers. But the extent to which they can subordinate these in order to experience their customers without evaluating them will play a large part in determining their success.

5. *Analyze.* It is a good idea to teach your salespeople to record their customer and organizational observations in a diary, which can serve as their intelligence file. In it they can record their current perceptions of the individual strengths and weaknesses of key decision makers and influencers along with their blind spots, hypersensitive areas, personality traits, preferences and aversions, overt and hidden power lines, and other important data. For each customer department or division, they can make a simple network diagram which connects each key customer to his organizational supporters, antagonists, and neutrals. They can also chart the interactions between customer departments as well as who relates to whom and how. Fortified with such basic intelligence information, they will have a stronger base from which to create successful selling strategies.

TEACH HOW TO PROFILE
A CUSTOMER'S COGNITIVE STYLE

To read a customer, the first step your salespeople must be taught is to diagnose his cognitive style. This will enable them to learn how their customer receives, processes, stores, and utilizes the information that composes his frame of reference. Four aspects of cognitive style are important for your salespeople to learn how to analyze. Two of these aspects are relatively simple to understand: the customer's *speed of comprehension* and whether his *intellectual focus* is on abstract ideas, practical problems, or people. Two other aspects of cognitive style are more complicated. They are the customer's cognitive complexity and his cognitive structure.

Cognitive complexity. Some customers' thought processes are simple; others are more complex. Three kinds of cognitive structure are useful to distinguish:

> *Simplistic.* Prefers either-or thought patterns, with information processed in polar opposite terms such as good and bad.
> *Orderly.* Prefers disciplined thought patterns, with data sorted according to traditional categories.
> *Complex.* Prefers to analyze data across a wide range of subtleties and nuances.

Cognitive structure. Customers differ in their cast of mind. Some are verbally oriented while others are primarily figure oriented. One may be thoughtful and reflective while another will be unconventional and action oriented.

Teach your salespeople to construct a *cognitive style profile* for each decision-making customer. Use Figure 10-1 as a model in profiling each customer's cognitive style according to 17 criteria which are helpful in understanding him.

TEACH HOW TO PROFILE
A CUSTOMER'S CONATIVE TENDENCIES

Customers are striving, seeking, acquisitive individuals. They are always doing something to satisfy their needs. There are six aspects of customer purchase behavior that you should teach your salespeople to bear in mind: (1) Purchase behavior is always caused and never random. (2) It is always goal-directed, even when its objective seems obscure. (3) It is always tension-reducing in the short run, even when it may

Figure 10–1
Cognitive style profile.

CUSTOMER NAME _____

CUSTOMER'S COGNITIVE STYLE	ABOVE AVERAGE	AVERAGE	BELOW AVERAGE

1. *Intellectual Preference*

   Abstractions

   Concrete situations

   Social situations

2. *Cognitive Complexity*

   Simplistic

   Orderly

   Complex

3. *Cognitive Orientation*

   Language

   Numbers

   People

   Ideas

4. *Cognitive Movement*

   Slow and plodding

   Fast-paced

   Unconventional

   Conservative and cautious

   Imaginative and creative

   Thoughtful and reflective

5. *Evaluative Capacity*

create greater difficulty over the long term. (4) It always seeks either to increase need satisfaction or to avoid decreasing it. (5) It is never the result of only one drive or need. (6) It always appears perfectly reasonable to the customer.

Since all customer behavior is need-satisfying in purpose, you should familiarize your salespeople with two major theories of need: Maslow's theory and the approaches of McClelland and White.

Maslow's theory. You remember that A. H. Maslow[1] has organized five human needs as a hierarchy, ranging from physiological needs such as food and clothing through security needs, social needs, ego needs for achievement and respect, to self-actualization needs. Maslow's hierarchy of needs suggests seven applications by your salespeople with their customers.

1. A sales representative can motivate a customer only by appealing to the pattern of his needs that is currently dominant.
2. A customer will usually want a balanced satisfaction of all his needs rather than the maximum satisfaction of any single need.
3. Once a customer's need is satisfied, it will no longer motivate him.
4. Customer behavior is generally multimotivated.
5. Lower-level customer needs are the easiest to meet.
6. Most customers tend to emphasize the satisfaction of their higher-level needs.
7. Customers are insatiable as far as their need satisfaction is concerned. This is why customers always ask, "What have you done for me lately?"

McClelland's and White's approaches. David McClelland and R. W. White approach customers as achievers, people who are striving for accomplishment.[2] They divide customers

---

[1] A. H. Maslow, *Motivation and Personality* (New York: Harper & Row, 1954).

[2] D. C. McClelland, *The Achieving Society* (Princeton, N.J.: D. Van Nostrand, 1961); R. W. White, "Motivation Reconsidered: The Concept of Competence," *Psychological Review*, Vol. 66, No. 5, 1959.

into success seekers and failure avoiders. Success seekers prefer situations where the risk of failure is neither too great nor too small. They are motivated more by the prospect of achievement than by fear of failing. Failure avoiders prefer sure things to chancy ones. They like situations that are predictable rather than those where luck, chance, or external variables play a considerable role in determining the outcome.

Teach your salespeople to construct a *conative tendency profile* for each decision-making customer. Use Figure 10-2 as a model in profiling each customer's conative tendencies according to 23 criteria which are helpful to understanding him.

TEACH HOW TO PROFILE A CUSTOMER'S SOCIAL AND EMOTIONAL CHARACTERISTICS

A customer's social and emotional characteristics play an important role in determining the type of relationship that a salesman can create with him. Some customers will move toward a salesman quickly and easily. Others hang back or move away. A few may even put up resistance. These social tendencies have their origin in customer personality structure.

Teach your salesmen to construct social and emotional characteristics profiles for each decision-making customer. Use Figures 10-3 and 10-4 as models in profiling each customer's characteristics according to 26 criteria which are helpful to understanding him.

TEACH HOW TO PROFILE A CUSTOMER'S ATTITUDES

An *attitude* is a predisposition to feel or act in a certain way. Sometimes it is called a mental set, indicating that the mind is set to go in a certain direction. You should teach your salespeople to keep in mind the following six characteristics of the attitudes their customers can bring to a sales relationship with them.

(Please turn to page 131.)

Figure 10–2
Conative tendency profile.

CUSTOMER NAME _____

CUSTOMER'S CONATIVE STYLE	ABOVE AVERAGE	AVERAGE	BELOW AVERAGE
Need for:			
1. Power			
2. Dominance over others			
3. Affiliation			
4. Control of the situation			
5. Achievement			
6. Attention			
7. Increased competence			
8. Ego-building responses			
9. Aggression			
10. Deference from others			
11. Status and prestige			
12. Independence			
13. Recognition			
14. Sense of adequacy			
15. Sense of self-esteem			
16. Dependence			
17. Success			
18. Failure avoidance			
19. Risk-taking			
20. Closeness with others			
21. Social distance from others			
22. Hostility			
23. Interaction with others			

Figure 10–3
Social characteristics profile.

CUSTOMER NAME _____

CUSTOMER'S SOCIAL CHARACTERISTICS	BELOW AVERAGE	AVERAGE	ABOVE AVERAGE
1. Tendency to move toward others			
2. Tendency to move against others			
3. Tendency to move away from others			
4. Other-directed tendencies			
5. Inner-directed tendencies			

Figure 10–4
Emotional characteristics profile.

CUSTOMER NAME _____

1. Open and authentic _____ Secretive
   1 2 3 4 5

2. Emotionally mature _____ Lacking in self-control
   1 2 3 4 5

3. Self-sufficient _____ Dependent
   1 2 3 4 5

4. Cooperative _____ Exploitative
   1 2 3 4 5

5. Self-objective _____ Self-blind
   1 2 3 4 5

6. Cautious _____ Venturesome
   1 2 3 4 5

Figure 10–4 (continued)

7. Considerate   _____   Self-centered

       1   2   3   4   5

8. Conservative   _____   Liberal

       1   2   3   4   5

9. Friendly   _____   Antagonistic

       1   2   3   4   5

10. Energetic   _____   Passive

       1   2   3   4   5

11. Even-tempered   _____   Moody, changeable

       1   2   3   4   5

12. Gregarious   _____   Introverted

       1   2   3   4   5

13. Conventional   _____   Unconventional

       1   2   3   4   5

14. Self-assured   _____   Timid

       1   2   3   4   5

15. Predictable   _____   Erratic

       1   2   3   4   5

16. Positive-minded   _____   Negativistic

       1   2   3   4   5

17. Cooperative   _____   Aggressive

       1   2   3   4   5

18. Independent-minded   _____   Conforming

       1   2   3   4   5

19. Future-oriented   _____   Past-oriented

       1   2   3   4   5

20. Spontaneous   _____   Reserved

       1   2   3   4   5

21. Inner-directed   _____   Other-directed

       1   2   3   4   5

1. Attitudes are remarkably stable. Once formed, they are very difficult to change.
2. Attitudes defy logic. They often exist simply because they exist.
3. A customer may have contradictory attitudes.
4. Attitudes underlie a customer's motivation.
5. Attitudes determine a customer's perception of the sales representative and the relationship between them.
6. Attitudes cannot be reasoned with. An appeal to reason gains little or nothing in altering an attitude.

Your salespeople must learn to detect a customer's attitudes even though the customer will rarely proclaim them openly. You can teach them to find major cues from customer behavior. A second set of cues can come from a customer's communication, especially what he connotes by leaving unsaid. Chance comments, so-called offhand remarks which are really on-hand, silent comments through body language, jokes, and opinions or evaluations which seemingly refer to others can reveal customer preferences and aversions. A third set of cues can come from a customer's expressed ideas about issues, groups, and individuals.

Teach your salesmen to construct an attitude profile for each decision-making customer. Use Figure 10-5 as a model for profiling each customer's attitudes which are helpful in understanding him.

TEACH THE PRINCIPLES OF
PERCEPTIVE ORGANIZATION PROFILING

Teaching your salespeople how to map the organization structure of their heavy-user customers will enable them to broaden and deepen their penetration so as to reach the primary decision makers and their influencers who control your sales.

In order for your salespeople to be able to move easily through their customer organizations, you will have to teach them how to map six systems within each customer business:(1) power system, (2) influence system, (3) political system, (4) value system, (5) role system, and, (6) group system.

131

Figure 10–5
Attitude profile.

CUSTOMER NAME   _____

Positive attitudes
  (Preferences)

_____

_____

_____

_____

_____

_____

Negative attitudes
  (Aversions)

_____

_____

_____

_____

_____

_____

Every customer is part of the culture medium of his organization. The organization is also part of the customer. A purchasing agent, design engineer, or product manager is a spokesman for a complex group of organizational pushes and pulls. As buying committees, audit committees, and steering committees grow in popularity among companies, the independence of each individual member diminishes because his own traits, values, and attitudes become colored by others. It is essential for your salespeople to know who these other influencers and decision makers are as well as what personal and organizational points of view they represent.

It is therefore necessary for you to teach your salespeople to profile their customer organizations. Every organization presents two faces to a sales representative. One is the face of the apparent organization, represented by the paper logic of its organization chart, position descriptions, policy statements, and programmed activities. This is the face your salespeople must penetrate. They must get through to the real face of the organization, which mirrors its political power structure and the mix of pseudo-friendships, covert jealousies, uneasy alliances, and complex interpersonal roles which compose it.

If your salespeople are to become organizationally perceptive, they will need to profile the six systems within each customer organization, as cited earlier. Each of these systems is one aspect of an organization's decision-making mechanism; each will carry a different weight of importance for almost every company. In a small organization, one aspect may rule. In larger companies, several can be dominant.

To prepare your salespeople to profile these six aspects of a customer company, use Figure 10-6 to analyze its organization structure according to eight characteristics which are helpful in understanding it.

1. Teach How to Profile a Power System

Power is the ability to impose will. In a customer organization, a person's power can be perceived by the number of options open to him and his freedom to choose the one he wants. The more numerous the options and the freer the choice among them, the greater the power.

Power in many customer organizations is difficult to perceive. For one thing, it is fragmented. No one has it all. Almost everyone has some. Very few have none. For another thing, power is limited. The more one man has, the less there is to go around. Furthermore, power is rarely delegated. It is generally grasped rather than awarded. A fourth fact about power is probably the most difficult to deal with. Power comes in several varieties. One kind can approve action and get things done. Another kind can veto action and keep things

Figure 10–6
Organization structure analysis.

COMPANY NAME _____

CHARACTERISTIC	CHECK ONE	ANALYSIS
1. Climate		
Autocratic	_____	_____
Paternalistic	_____	_____
Bureaucratic	_____	_____
Democratic	_____	_____
2. Decision Makers		
Improvers and innovators	_____	_____
Maintainers and storekeepers	_____	_____
Failure avoiders	_____	_____
MBO-oriented	_____	_____
Tradition-routine bound	_____	_____
3. Self-Image		
Risk-taking and creative	_____	_____
Industry leader	_____	_____
Conservative and traditional	_____	_____
Maturely sophisticated	_____	_____
4. Tempo		
Fast-paced	_____	_____
Impulsive and erratic	_____	_____
Planful and deliberate	_____	_____
Slow-moving and change-resistant	_____	_____

Figure 10–6 (continued)

CHARACTERISTIC	CHECK ONE	ANALYSIS
5. Communication Patterns		
Free and open	_____	_____
Defensive and secretive	_____	_____
Guarded, formal, and polite	_____	_____
Downward imperative	_____	_____
6. Decision-Making Process		
One-man	_____	_____
Top in-group	_____	_____
Specialist group	_____	_____
Collaborative and participative	_____	_____
7. Company Personality		
Task-oriented	_____	_____
Improvement-oriented	_____	_____
Status-quo-oriented	_____	_____
Conflicted and exploitative	_____	_____
Suspicious	_____	_____
Cooperative	_____	_____
8. Tone of Key Personnel		
Conforming and apathetic	_____	_____
Distrustful of one another	_____	_____
Dependent, fearful	_____	_____
Achieving and success-seeking	_____	_____
Self-aggrandizing	_____	_____

135

from getting done. A third kind can mediate between the other two.

Position power. Every title carries an electrical charge. Many titles appear more highly charged than they really are. Sometimes titles are bestowed in place of power. A truly powerful decision maker is a sales representative's best customer. Together thay can make plans that carry a high level of confidence about being converted into action.

Expert power. Many a decision maker is merely authorizing the recommendations of other people in the organization who possess an expert power on which he is almost wholly dependent.

Referent power. The most personal kind of power in an organization is the referent power possessed by influencers. These are people whose recommendations are esteemed enough to be listened to and incorporated into action by the holders of position power. Pinpointing influencers is one of the most important tasks confronting a salesperson. If he pinpoints wrong, he risks the loss of time, effort, and money. By pinpointing correctly, he can add a major asset to his selling relationship.

There are two keystones to teach your salesforce for profiling a customer organization's power system.

1. Identify the different kinds of clout in a customer organization. First, find out who has *power over.* They can compel others. Then find out who has *power to.* They can affect what is done. Finally, identify those who have *power in.* They can exert power in certain situations even though their power is otherwise quite limited. If the situation is right for them, they can often be the most helpful of all.

2. Correlate titles with actual power. A title may equal only paper power. No title gives its holder all kinds of power.

Teach your salespeople to construct an organization power system profile for each customer company. Use Figure 10-7 as a model. On it, one company's power holders can be identified along with the kind of power each one carries, its source, and how it is exercised. Then have your salespeople compare this power chart against their customers' formal organization charts to correlate title power with actual power.

Figure 10–7
Organization power system profile.

COMPANY NAME _____

POWER HOLDERS	KIND OF POWER	HOW EXERCISED

2. Teach How to Profile an Influence System

Power is grasped, but influence must be gained. Influence can sometimes be a form of personal power. In every customer organization, some influencers are also decision makers. Other influencers make no decisions themselves but give a decision maker his dominant direction.

There are three keystones to teach your salespeople about profiling a customer organization's influence system.

1. Identify the members of the customer organization who appear to interact on a frequent and recurrent basis.

2. Note which people initiate these interactions most often. Note also who the repetitive responders are.

3. Remember the people or departments that are typically represented by customers as checkpoints or referral stations to which proposals must go for screening and recommendation before they can be acted on.

Teach your salespeople to construct an organization influence system profile for each customer company. Using Figure 10-8 as a model, have each salesperson identify one customer company's influencers together with the decision makers who refer to them and the areas for decision on which they counsel.

3. Teach How to Profile a Political System

A customer company's political system complements its formal organization. The formal organization allows its members to achieve corporate objectives. The political system allows them to reach their personal objectives.

You must teach your salespeople to be both aware and wary of their customer organization's political system. Their awareness will sensitize them to learning which politicians already hold office and which are quietly running for election. Their wariness will help them to remain prudent observers and avoid taking sides.

There are four keystones to teach your salesforce about profiling a customer organization's political system.

1. Identify the members of the customer organization who have organizational power. Next, identify those who have

Figure 10–8
Organization influence system profile.

COMPANY NAME _____

INFLUENCERS	DECISION MAKERS WHO ARE INFLUENCED	AREAS FOR DECISION

political power. Correlate the two groups. Mark for special attention the customers who have both kinds of power as well as those who have political power without equally important stature in their organizations.

2. Locate the next potential political in-group. At the same time, label each out-group.

3. Make note of common interests which could cause the in-group to join forces with an out-group. Also note the situations in which two or more out-groups might find common cause.

4. Sketch out the circumstances in which an out-group could become the in-group and the in-group an out-group. List the probable effects of such a flip-flop on the selling climate.

Teach your salespeople to construct an organization political system profile for each customer company. Using Figure 10-9 as a model, have each member of the salesforce show the interrelations between one customer company's organization and its political power groups.

4. Teach How to Profile a Value System

Every customer company has its own value system. It places importance on certain principles and premises by assuming them to be more or less eternal truths. Values are rarely committed to writing. Instead, they are communicated informally from person to person. In this way, your customers come to know that they are their organization's kind of people and that there is a "right way" to do things.

You must teach your salespeople to regard their customers' value systems as *codes of ethics*. Whether or not a salesperson agrees with or even approves of these value systems, he must respect them. Since the value system sets a customer organization's self-image, each salesperson must correlate his own image with its most important aspects if he wants to be identified with customer values.

There are three keystones to teach your salespeople about a customer organization's value system.

1. Define the predominant values that the organization professes. For example, note whether it stresses innovation

Figure 10–9
Organization political system profile.

COMPANY NAME _____

NAME   ORGANIZATION TITLE   POLITICAL POWER

Figure 10–10
Organization value system profile.

COMPANY NAME _____

APPROVED VALUES   DISAPPROVED VALUES

_____   _____

_____   _____

_____   _____

_____   _____

_____   _____

or stability, the achievement of success or the avoidance of failure.

2. Evaluate the extent to which the organization practices decentralized profit responsibility, functional or divisional autonomy, and the delegation of individual decision making rather than centralized committee rule.

3. Determine what constitutes esteemed, tolerated, and forbidden behavior.

Teach your salespeople to construct an organization value system profile for each customer company, using Figure 10-10 as a model. On it, have each salesman show one customer company's approved and disapproved values.

5. Teach How to Profile a Role System

Roles are behavior styles. When a customer plays the role of customer, he acts out of a mixture of two converging forces. The first is his own self-perceived role in which he expresses his concept of what a customer does and how he does it. This concept is usually a synthesis of the conversational and action styles of several role models who have been the customer's managers or peers. The second is his role as others in the organization have let him know they perceive it. A customer's perception that he holds a tough job often convinces him that he must act like a tough customer who gives salespeople a hard time.

There are three keystones to teach your salesforce about profiling a customer organization's role system.

1. Identify the roles played by each decision maker and influencer in a customer organization. Identify, too, the *role expectations* they have about how salespeople should act toward them. Correlate each role with the role player's position, power, and values.

2. Define the types of role conflict which decision makers and influencers seem to be having. Note the effects they have on sales decisions.

3. Identify the members of a customer organization who use their power to impose defensive roles on salespeople.

Teach your salespeople to construct an organization role system profile for each customer company. Using Figure 10-11 as a model, have each salesperson choose one customer company and show the role each decision maker prefers to play with him and the corresponding role he is expected to play in return.

6. Teach How to Profile a Group System

In most decision-making situations, the decisive unit is not an individual but a group. A group is two or more people who interact in such a way as to provide "rewards" and assess "costs" for one another. The group may be a buying committee, screening committee, audit committee, or other formal selection committee, or it may be informal. Because individuals act in different ways when they are part of a group, you must teach your salespeople to know the groupings in their customer organizations which can affect them.

In many instances, groups can reinforce an individual customer's decision. They can also negate it. Groups work through social pressure. They set their own norms, impose standards, reward and punish loners and nonconformists, and can enforce attitude and behavior changes by their members.

Every group, whether formal or informal, has its own
(Please turn to page 147.)

Figure 10—11
Organization role system profile.

COMPANY NAME _____

DECISION-MAKER'S NAME	PREFERRED ROLE	CORRESPONDING ROLE FOR ME
	Partner in problem definition and solution	
	Shrewd bargainer	
	Obstacle builder	
	Fault-finding critic	
	Collaborative negotiator	
	Decision maker	
	Decision coordinator	
	Forceful initiator	
	Cooperative follower	
	Spokesman for company needs	

Spokesman for self-centered wants _____

Help seeker _____

Help provider _____

Answer seeker _____

Answer provider _____

Aggressive attacker _____

Defensive counterpuncher _____

Salesman supporter _____

Constructive participant _____

Pleader for special exceptions _____

Figure 10–12
Organization group system profile.

TYPE OF GROUP _____

SOURCE OF INTERACTION   GROUP MEMBERS

Possess expert power   _____

Have referent power and
   influence with the group   _____

Have the ear of superiors   _____

Exert influence in other
   departments   _____

Are listened to by the members of
   other groups   _____

Usually band together   _____

Generally are opposed to each
   other   _____

Serve as spokesmen for the
   company's ideas and feelings   _____

Usually adopt leadership roles   _____

Generally adopt followership
   roles   _____

Often come up with the most
   creative ideas   _____

Frequently come up with effective
   practical strategies for getting
   things done   _____

Try to manipulate the group   _____

Go their own way and "march to
   their own drummer"   _____

Are most respected by other group
   members   _____

Figure 10–12 (continued)

Usually serve as mediators and
conciliators of opposing views

_____

Usually cause trouble and friction
within the company

_____

Have a reputation for knowing
what will take place

_____

Know how to make changes within
the system without making
waves

_____

personality, customs, and unwritten laws. Each has its own sensitivities. Groups find ways of relating to one another. They have their own internal pecking order and external status ranking. In many customer organizations, the informal groups rule. Your salespeople must be able to seek them out and penetrate their deliberations, either personally or through the mediation of an internal influencer. In this way, they can participate in the most important decisions which affect their customer relationships.

There are four keystones to teach your salesforce about profiling a customer organization's group system.

1. Identify the major deciding groups, both formal and informal. Assign each group a rank order of pressure which it can exert on the others.

2. Specify the reactions which pressured groups use to withstand pressure or turn it around.

3. Make note of group leaders, especially those who lead both formal and informal groups.

4. Classify the decisions that come out of each kind of group. Understand the decision areas where formal and informal groups work in harmony or where their decisions thwart each other or cancel each other out.

Teach your salespeople to construct an organization group system profile for each customer company. Using Figure 10–12 as a model, have each one choose a customer company and construct a group interaction profile for each kind of group.

11
How to teach customer negotiation

Teaching your salespeople how to sell by using the process of negotiation means that they will be freed from relying on persuasion and high-pressure selling and be able to use customer need fulfillment as their basic sales platform. Once customer needs have been established, your salesforce will have to be able to employ four basic negotiation strategies: (1) cooperative strategies, (2) accommodative strategies, (3) defensive strategies, and (4) assertive strategies.

Negotiation is the act of bargaining with customers to reach win-win objectives: objectives which enable customers to win premium values and at the same time enable your salespeople to win a premium price. Win-win relationships are the only ones in which salespeople and customers can be equals.

In order to negotiate, your salespeople must reject two other customer relationships.

1. The "I win, you lose" relationship is based on each salesperson's ability to persuade the customers that he knows the solutions to customer problems better than the customers do and therefore has the right to impose solutions on customers.

2. The "you win, I lose" relationship is based on a salesperson's ability to manage a philanthropy rather than a business,

BENEFITS OF NEGOTIATION

Negotiation offers five benefits over and above the values of persuasion, compromise, and accommodation. First, negotiation better serves a customer's personal and professional needs for *recognition as an individual.* When your sales representative negotiates with a customer, he is implicitly acknowledging the customer's need to have his purposes served. Each person is enhanced by the selling process. Another way to say the same thing is to note that the two of them are equalized by negotiation; that is, they are positioned as peers, important to themselves and to each other, and therefore capable of becoming partners.

A second benefit of negotiation is the way it contributes to the climate of confidence your salespeople must create in their key account relationships. When they negotiate with a customer, they demonstrate that they are not out to use him merely as a means to their own ends. This enables the typical salesman-customer you-and-me relationship to mature into a we-and-our relationship in which the customer can have confidence that the salesperson's proposals are in the customer's best interest.

Negotiation is the bargaining process which is preferred by salespeople who include the added value of their personal applications expertise to the products and services they sell. This permits them to position themselves in an advisory and counseling relationship with their customers. From this posi-

149

tion, they can apply their products and services as means of improving their customer's profit. This is a third benefit of negotiation.

A fourth benefit can be derived from the information exchange which negotiation encourages through its give-and-take dialogues. As your salespeople negotiate, their customers are exposed to a wide range of knowledge about your company, your product and service benefits, and their effects on customer profitability. Customers can also learn how well your salespeople know their business problems and opportunities. In turn, your salespeople can learn more about customer problems, how they rank in priority order of paying attention to them, and what political, organizational, or financial constraints may stand in the way of taking action on them.

A fifth benefit of negotiation is that it is conducive to establishing a long-term relationship as a customer's preferred supplier. Negotiation avoids many of the conflicts that are likely to short-circuit a promising relationship. Unlike persuasion and compromise, which frequently contain the seeds of future conflict because they leave a residue of unfulfilled needs, negotiation can help build a stable relationship which resists self-destruction as well as competitive inroads.

DISTINGUISHING NEGOTIATION FROM PERSUASION, ACCOMMODATION, AND COMPROMISE

Many of your salespeople will think they are negotiating when they are really not negotiating. They may not know the difference or care to admit it. But their customers do. You should know what the differences are between negotiation and other sales strategies that are more accurately classified as persuasion, accommodation, and compromise. There is nothing wrong with using these approaches when they properly apply. Each has its role. But they should not be mistaken for negotiation.

How Persuasion Differs from Negotiation

Persuasion is a you-win strategy that can be a useful element of negotiation. But negotiation is not persuasion by another name. Persuasion implies the subtle imposition of a seller's will on the customer in order to win him over, prevail over his objections, and bring him around to the salesperson's thinking. Persuasion at best can achieve only reluctant submission rather than wholehearted agreement. Moreover, when persuasion is used habitually, it can create a number of problems.

1. It connotes that the seller knows what is best for the customer. This is a risky assumption.

2. It makes the seller appear psychologically superior to the customer, who then becomes suspicious that he may be manipulated into purchase.

3. Persuasion implies that the seller is seeking to use the customer for the seller's own ends.

4. Once persuaded does not mean always persuaded. When a customer has had time to think things over there may be a boomerang effect. Thus at times persuasion may actually be counterproductive.

5. If the seller fails to provide the customer with countervailing arguments against later persuaders, the most recent persuader may get the customer's business.

How Accommodation Differs from Negotiation

Accommodation is another one-winner strategy. One party must be superior. The other party must therefore be inferior. In essence, accommodation is unilateral: only the customer is expected to accommodate. The alternative is that the salesperson must give in.

Once the salesperson gives in, he will face even greater difficulty the next time he tries to hold fast against accommodating his customer. If he keeps giving in, he may reach a point where he becomes so resilient that he seems more like a piece of cooked spaghetti than a professional salesperson. As a professional, he must *profess* a clear, consistent integrity. This customer has the same mission. If either of them accommodates the other too often under pressure, both may find themselves losing their sense of integrity.

How can you help your salespeople determine the limits within which they can safely accommodate? You can teach them the four major guides. The first is their convictions. The second guide is the policies and practices of your company. Private deals at the company's expense have no place in negotiation. The third guide is your company's image. Accommodation is poor strategy if it puts your organization in a negative light in the eyes of your customers. The fourth guide is that your salespeople must learn to maximize the satisfying benefits and advantages which your customers will derive from dealing with them and which often make accommodation unnecessary.

How Compromise Differs from Negotiation

Compromise is a nobody-wins strategy. Even though the only way to close a sale may often require that both the salesperson and his customer give up something neither wants to yield, compromise carries with it at least five important limitations.

1. It may result in a solution that is acceptable but not really satisfying to either party. Each feels that he has sacrificed something he really wanted to achieve. Compromise often gives only temporary relief because each party to the compromise feels cheated.

2. It may prompt a sales representative and his customer to be suspicious of each other. In every compromise, each party is forced to be wary of the "opponent" and to be on guard lest he be outwitted and taken in.

3. Compromise often makes it necessary for a salesperson and his customer to play games. Each may anticipate the eventual need to compromise by starting out with outlandish demands. They may even find themselves threatening each other. In all compromises, hidden agendas dominate the proceedings. Second-guessing and maneuvering become the accepted way of relating.

4. Compromise makes agreement very hard to come by. Both parties want to get as much as possible while giving up as little as necessary. Time can be wasted. Energy is consumed unproductively. It is the nature of compromise to resort to tactics that alienate by making insistent demands or taking unyielding stands.

152

5. Compromise forces each party to be self-oriented, self-insistent, self-centered, and perhaps even self-indulgent, Small wonder that many compromises must in time be renegotiated.

TYPICAL CUSTOMER SITUATIONS FOR NEGOTIATION

Customer selling situations where negotiation strategies should be applied can be broken out into three types, as summarized in Figure 11-1. The first type is customer *complaints*. They usually involve problems concerning price, product performance, or company policy. The second type is customer *requests* for special treatment or consideration in product specifications, credit, or a variety of services. The third type of customer negotiation situation concerns *innovations*. These include the introduction of any important new policy, practice, products, or services into your customer relationships. When you have a new product to be introduced, your salesforce will normally require a good deal of educational negotiation to move it into its distribution channels and push it through to the customers. Much of this negotiation takes the form of an information transfer between salespeople and customers. When you must allocate a product or a material or alter its delivery schedules or its price, or when your salespeople must renegotiate a deal they thought they had sewed up with a customer, negotiation strategies are often the best bet.

Among the three customer negotiation situations, complaints are generally the most difficult. They require your salespeople to adopt defensive strategies before they can turn the situation around to a cooperative negotiation. On the other hand, customer requests will probably be the easiest to convert into business opportunities. A request is always a signal for help.

In most normal sales relationships, the third negotiation situation—innovations—should be the most prevalent. New product introductions, allocations, price and delivery date changes, competitive threats or simply the prospect of competitive threats, and the promotion, transfer, or retirement

153

Figure 11–1
Customer selling situations.

1. *Complaints*
    1.1. Price exceeds perceived value
    1.2. Product fails to perform according to promise
    1.3. Policy must be defended

2. *Requests*
    2.1. Product specifications must be customer-tailored
    2.2. Credit must be extended
    2.3. Service must be applied
    2.4. Unsold merchandise or discontinued models must be returned
    2.5. Advertising and sales promotion support must be provided
    2.6. Market research support must be provided
    2.7. Price concession must be granted
    2.8. Nearby inventory must be established
    2.9. Claims must be settled
    2.10. Product application education must be provided

3. *Innovations*
    3.1. New product must be introduced
    3.2. Product must be put on allocation
    3.3. Delivery must be speeded up or delayed
    3.4. Price increase must be justified
    3.5. Leasing terms must be set
    3.6. Competitive threat must be counteracted
    3.7. Self-manufacture must be discouraged
    3.8. Contract must be renegotiated with a new negotiator

of customer decision makers are characteristic events in customer relationships, where constant change is the rule. Negotiation is designed to preserve the stability of customer relationships in the face of change. Some of these situations will be initiated by customers. For example, they may come to you with threats of competitive inroads on your participation in their business. This innovation will require your salespeople to negotiate a defense until they can restore a cooperative situation. At other times, you yourself will initiate innovations that introduce change into customer relationships. In these situations, you will have to teach your salesforce to apply cooperative negotiation strategies.

SOLVING COMMON NEGOTIATION PROBLEMS

The three basic events which require customer negotiation—customer requests or complaints and innovations which can be introduced into your relationship by either of you—recur because they are inherent in selling. They are, from a human relations point of view, integral parts of the sale. Because they repeat themselves time after time with every customer, certain problems can confidently be predicted to occur. Based on experience, you can anticipate these negative circumstances before they happen and teach your salespeople how to react so that their negotiation strategies will take on an enhanced likelihood of success.

There are a few problem situations which are virtually common denominators in all customer–salesman relations. Four are concerned with your product: samples, modifications, callbacks and returns, and allocation. Two are concerned with certain aspects of your salespeople's performance on a day-to-day basis and when they are proposing. Two more are concerned with price and credit or finance. The final two problem situations have to do with promotional support services and dealer or distributor relations.

Solving Problems in Product Situations

1. *Sampling.* When your sales representative receives a customer request for a sample, a product prototype, or a trial installation, teach him not to give it away. Have him trade it off by negotiating for a commitment from his customer. Or have him trade it off for some information, especially a knowledge of competitive sampling policies. Even when he has made such a win–win tradeoff, still don't let him give the sample away. Teach him to quantify its dollar cost and make sure his customer perceives the value he is receiving by the fulfillment of his request. Also make sure your sales

representative knows the identity of the decision maker or influencer who is making the sample request so he can be included in future coverage of the account.

2. *Modifications.* In handling customer requests for product modifications, there are two pitfalls to be avoided. One is acquiescing too readily without first determining the need for a modification or for the particular modification requested, or without correlating the projected benefits from the modification with what is known about customer market needs. The other pitfall is to create a conflict situation by taking a negative stand at the outset and rejecting any consideration of a product change. Before your salespeople come to a point of view, teach them to talk to their customers' engineers, manufacturing people, sales managers, product managers, and anyone else who may be involved. Have the salespeople find out what the others think before saying what they themselves think. Then, if your salespeople decide to negotiate, have them call on your company's technical assistance before they commit to modification.

3. *Callbacks and returns.* To convert a product return request into a negotiable situation that offers your salespeople the opportunity to win something, teach them to make a hard resell effort in tradeoff. Have them research in depth the reasons their customers give for requesting return. Don't let them contest these requests until their validity has been probed. If the requests are incontestable, teach salespeople to learn from them and pass the learning along to you and your technical people. If a customer has been forced to make a callback of his own products because of product failure on your part, add to your sales representative's negotiating position an offer to help find a new market or other use for the customer's returns.

4. *Allocation.* Allocation requires early warning. If you notify your customers at a time that they perceive as late in their own planning cycle, your salespeople will immediately be put in a defensive and perhaps even indefensible position. When you must present an allocation notice, prepare a fact sheet with your salespeople stating why it is necessary, what its terms are, and how long its probable duration may be. Teach your salesforce to demonstrate empathy for customer

problems. The watchword is, be helpful. This means suggesting substitute materials or alternate suppliers. You may have to allocate your product but your salespeople don't have to hold back on consultative aid and comfort.

Solving Problems in Performance Situations

1. *Account handling.* If your salespeople discover a deficiency in their handling of a customer's business, teach them to do two things. First, remedy it. Second, communicate their discovery and its remedy to their customers. Don't have them announce their discovery without having a remedy prepared or, even better, already installed. If they attempt to cover up their deficiency, they will be hard-pressed to negotiate a defense if it surfaces. Stonewalling as a defense is not a negotiation strategy that will partner your salespeople and their customers. The best defense of an account-handling error of omission or commission, of course, is to make changes before problems occur. This is a leadership strategy. It allows your salespeople to quantify the dollar value of their innovation in return-on-investment terms. It also allows them to stress that their service is custom-tailored, which will help them brand it as distinct from competition.

2. *Proposal rejection.* When a customer rejects a proposal, he is actually making a request of his salesman: Understand my needs better and react to them more fittingly. He is, in effect, inviting the sales representative to be innovative and come back to him with a new approach. If you teach your salespeople to understand this attitude, you and they will be able to use rejection as the basis for negotiation, not withdrawal or persuasion for the customer to accept their proposals anyway. Instead of attempting to resell the original proposal, teach your salespeople to trade off rejection for an improved learning of customer needs. This can give them the opportunity to gain access to decision makers and influencers they might not otherwise be able to contact. Their revised proposals will then contain customer thinking as well as their own as a jointly developed, and perhaps jointly beneficial, recommendation of improved profits.

Solving Problems in Money Situations

1. *Pricing.* Every time you tamper with your price list you alter your customers' perception of value. Price negotiations then become tests of your salespeople's belief in the combined value of their products and services, their personal expertise in applying them to improve their customer's profit, and the information base they have at their disposal to help them make successful applications. If they yield on price without trading off value, they can destroy the high value-to-price relationships they must maintain in order to command a premium. Where they have no unique value to trade for price, they run the risk of putting themselves in a commodity position where their customers will determine price. This means you should teach your salespeople two things. Have them justify price maintenance by added value. And when they must cut back in price, teach them to eliminate some of the value it represents so that they will not destroy their basic value-to-price relationship.

2. *Credit and finance.* A customer who requests credit is actually negotiating a form of price concession, which means that your value-to-price relationship will be confronted. Teach your salespeople to protect it by making their recommendation for a credit extension represent an added value of doing business with them. If they cannot trade off the added value at the moment, have them stockpile it for future use. Teach them to keep their customers informed of their role as the customer's agent in their internal negotiations with credit and collection people. Have them position themselves as their customers' partners. Encourage them to use their ability to provide credit as a justification for charging a premium price and achieving a favored supplier status.

Solving Problems in Dealer and Distributor Situations

When your customers sell importantly through dealers or distributors, you should consider them as a different level of customer. Remember that dealers and distributors are independent businessmen, probably much more entrepreneurial than your customers. This means that profit is necessarily the name of their game. Be sure you teach your salespeople to understand how their customers' products affect dealer or distributor profit and how they can help improve it. A sales representative can often improve his profitable sales volume considerably by helping a customer's dealers and distributors move more of your customer's products. He can do this best if he treats his customers' dealers and distributors as businessmen who have their own needs rather than simply as local sales outlets.

Solving Problems in Promotional Support Situations

Promotional support is a form of price concession. Therefore the same problem of maintaining your value-to-price relationship applies to requests for promotional support as it does to credit requests. If you provide free or cooperative customer support, teach your salespeople to trade it off for a value in return, especially for customer information. Put a value on the support services you provide in order to help your salespeople stockpile future trade-offs. If they cannot recommend free support for a customer, don't let them reject the request. Have them form partnerships to create no-cost support programs that customers can execute, such as tie-in sales, special events, seasonal promotions, and cooperative ventures with third parties.

TEACH HOW TO NEGOTIATE
BY CUSTOMER NEED-SEEKING

Your salespeople can negotiate with their customers only on the basis of seeking out and then helping to satisfy their needs. This process begins with the shared *development* of customer needs. It then moves on to a shared awareness of the needs, when salespeople and customers perceive the same needs with equal clarity. Finally, through shared fulfillment, your salespeople can accomplish their profit and sales objectives in the course of helping the customers realize their own profit objectives.

You must teach your salespeople to be developers of customer needs first and foremost. Customer needs are a salesman's raw materials. Negotiation is the process by which raw needs are refined and the solutions that are always within them can be distilled and packaged as sales proposals.

Needs are not developed easily because they are not revealed freely. A customer's needs are among his most proprietary possessions. It has been said that you don't learn needs—you earn the right to learn them. Because needs are so confidentially held, salespeople are rarely able to learn them swiftly or all at once. There are some needs they will never be able to discover in the most exacting, precise sense. The extent to which your salespeople can be perceived as consultants more than as suppliers will determine whether a climate of confidence can be created in which an interchange of need revelation and fulfillment can take place. Without these ingredients, there can never be a significant degree of confidence in a sales relationship. Where need revelation and fulfillment are not shared—where it becomes apparent to both seller and customer that the needs of only one of them are being met—the relationship will not endure. Two people will not long sustain a voluntary relationship that benefits only one of them.

Successful negotiation depends on your salespeople's ability to act as relationship builders with their customers. This aptitude is called *empathy*. It has also been called the salesman's bridge to his customer, the communication pathway that enables two people to work with each other in commitment to a single common objective. Empathy also has a feeling component. Unlike sympathy, which suggests a *feeling for* someone else, empathy enables a salesman to *feel with* his customers without becoming emotionally involved or blinded by their emotional frames of reference. The key to empathy is not to try to become the other person. On the contrary, it is to be very much oneself but to act, think, and feel with the other person so that the two can combine their powers to solve a common problem.

TEACH THE PRINCIPLES OF NEGOTIATION

To prepare your salespeople to become negotiators with their customers rather than persuaders or philanthropists, teach them the following seven principles of negotiation and have them incorporate these principles into their customer relationships.

1. Respect each customer. In turn, earn his respect. Be yourself so he can know the proper "you" to have respect for. Avoid trying to dominate the relationship so that both of you can value it equally.

2. Act like a consultant. This means substitute a teaching role for sales aggressiveness. The first thing to teach a customer is how to become a client. This means replacing his traditional customer defensiveness with a partnership approach that makes your work together take on the qualities of a joint venture.

3. Be open, intellectually accessible, and authentic. Disclose yourself and your motives to your customer. Start out by frankly and unashamedly admitting your self-interest in every transaction. Lay it on the line. In turn, allow the customer to reciprocate.

4. Set objectives that are agreeable to both of you. Once the ends are accepted, the strategic means can be worked out. Spell out clearly how achievement of the objectives will benefit each of you.

5. Be empathic about the customer's needs. Feel the situation from his perspective. Play it back to him as you feel it so he can validate your assumptions. Validation is the first step toward the successive agreements that must occur in customer negotiation.

6. Communicate in a way that advances the relationship by adding new insights and revelations and by reinforcing feedback. Discuss rather than debate.

7. Acknowledge each customer's need for his defense mechanisms. Don't try to beat your way through them or break them down. Create a relationship with him that will make many of his accustomed defenses unnecessary.

TEACH FOUR BASIC NEGOTIATION STRATEGIES

Of the four basic negotiation strategies—cooperative, accommodative, defensive, and assertive—you should teach your salespeople that they will always find it preferable to use cooperative negotiation strategies. But sometimes their customers won't let them. Then they will have to use accommodative strategies.

At other times, they will have to use defensive or assertive strategies. This can occur when their customers attempt to depersonalize them or manipulate them for their own purposes, prefer to keep the relationship ambiguous rather than secure, or keep testing the limits by pushing your salespeople as far as they can.

1. Cooperative Negotiation

1.1. *Make your customer an ally.* Seek to help your customer and let him know it. Use your complete array of company resources to create and widen areas of shared new learning between the two of you.

1.2. *Put your cards on the table.* Make it clear exactly what you can and cannot expect to accomplish. Make sure your expectations are the same since each of you will evaluate the relationship's success on how well they are met.

1.3. *Be patient.* Cultivate the ground, plant seeds of information and recommendation, and water them regularly. To attempt to harvest too soon may set the crop back by years. Always offer service in advance of asking for an order.

1.4. *Disagree when necessary,* but do so in the form of playing devil's advocate. This enables you to point out alternatives, project dire consequences, or tactfully indicate better ways of achieving objectives without directly confronting the customer's points of view.

1.5. *Build on your customer's real strengths.* Help optimize what he already has going for him. Supplement his weaknesses. Make him become good, not just look good. Since opportunity equals need plus capability, contribute your capability to the customer's need.

1.6. *Run behind your blockers.* Develop influencers inside the customer's organization who can block out opposition for you. Take time to make friends with the customer's subordinates, his associates, and even his superiors.

1.7. *Show extra effort.* Perform at a level that your

customer can perceive as being clearly above and beyond routine sales calling. This is especially important when the customer has a severe problem. Help him make lemonade out of his lemon.

2. Accommodative Negotiation

2.1. *Yield diagonally.* If a customer is insistent that you must accede to him or lose the sale, yield one or more slices rather than nothing or everything. Practice slow, limited withdrawal. Often, enough can be saved this way to justify the effort.

2.2. *Turn the other cheek.* If you and your customer are both aware that the customer is at fault in a situation, accept part of the blame so that he can save face. This will help him appreciate one of the principal benefits of his partnership with you.

2.3. *Learn when to leave well enough alone.* Forsake the goal of an ideal solution to every problem. There are times when the best policy is to take what the defense gives you.

2.4. *Bide your time.* It is often necessary to "go in the customer's door, though you fully intend to come out a door that is compatible to both of you." This may take time. At the opportune moment, regain the initiative. In negotiation, patience is a major virtue.

3. Defensive Negotiation

3.1. *Prevent showdowns.* If a customer initiates a confrontation, avoid allowing either of you to achieve a victory. If possible, avoid the battle entirely. In a situation that is going from bad to worse, it is sometimes wise to create a confrontation on your own terms. Position it as a shared learning experience and not a war.

3.2. *Stand pat.* Take a firm stand in the face of unreasonable demands. Don't boast about it. Define your position in factual terms. Frequently this will be sufficient, especially with a customer who is testing your boundaries to see how far you can be manipulated.

3.3. *Get lost.* If negotiation seems inopportune, try again another day. Adopt a low profile until the coast is clear. Come back when things are getting better after having been as bad as they can be.

3.4. *Destroy a straw man.* Give your customer a chance to work off aggression and win something by creating an attractive side issue that is relatively less important.

3.5. *Run the end.* Outflank a problem customer. Make allies with other people in his company. Use the buddy system with the customer as much as possible to avoid alienation.

3.6. *Counterattack.* Keep a few strategic options open for boomeranging back an unjustified allegation or assault on your position. This is sometimes called the *yes, but* strategy.

3.7. *Reverse your field.* Back up and start over. Become a moving target by taking several different tacks. Keep the situation unbalanced until it settles out.

3.8. *Make a tossed salad.* Periodically introduce new information into the negotiation. Focus discussion on the new information and stay away from the hot issues. This helps buy time.

3.9. *Keep sawing wood.* Stick to your plan and as much as possible ignore the customer's negative attitudes and counterproductive activities in the negotiation.

3.10. *Be up for adoption.* Induce the customer to join your side. Find a strong shared need such as helping him gain acceptance for your plans upstairs so that both of you can look good.

4. Assertive Negotiation

4.1. *Come in high.* Set initially high objectives and make high demands. After the trade-off you may end up with a greater payoff. By coming in high, you can condition the customer. Then, by letting him take advantage of the room you have left for compromise, you can recondition him.

4.2. *Trump his ace.* Let him seem able to go all the way with his proposal. Then tackle him at the goal line with an attractive counterproposal.

4.3. *Develop momentum.* Take initiative right from the start by setting the objectives and moving firmly toward them.

Force issues. Keep the pressure on. Once you grab a bull by the horns, don't let go.

4.4. *Surprise him.* Keep the customer off balance. Make him play "catch up." Use your information resources to stay one step ahead of the negotiation and pick apart his defenses.

4.5. *Acquire a sword or a shield.* Find a third party who favors your point of view and use him as a shield. Or find a third party who is depending on the customer's success for the achievement of his own objectives and who will act as a sword on your behalf.

4.6. *Carry a big stick.* If your ethical or operational boundaries are ignored or exceeded, threaten to withdraw or take an appeal upstairs. You can usually do this only once in a relationship.

THE CONCEPT OF PARTNERING

The basic concept of partnering is that partners do valuable things for each other. More accurately, partners *keep doing* valuable things for each other. If one partner stops doing things of value for the other, the partnership stops. A partnership can therefore be summed up at any time as an energy machine whose net worth is the total value of the things that are being done by it.

A rewarding partnership between a seller and a buyer has several valuable things going on within it all the time. In the first place, the partners are sharing in the achievement of a common objective. Most often, this objective is profit improvement for both. The customer improves his profit by having his costs cut or his sales revenues increased as a result of the salesperson's personal expertise in applying his products and services. The salesperson improves his profit by selling at a high price-to-value relationship.

The second major benefit which partners confer on each other is that they learn together. Their partnership is a breeding ground for new ideas which the partners generate together and put to work with shared wisdom, shared faith, and shared apprehension. Learning together how to improve profit is one of the strongest bonding agents in a customer–salesperson partnership. It vitalizes and continually renews the relationship because it is the growth element in the partnership. In an enduring relationship, both partners grow. When one partner learns more than the other, he outgrows the partnership.

A third key to partnership is that each partner complements the other. Each plays a supportive, supplementary role which divides the labor in the relationship according to each partner's capabilities. The complementary nature of the relationship enhances each of them. On the other hand, each partner is diminished by the absence of the other.

These three benefits—accomplishing shared objectives, learning together, and supporting and supplementing each other—are the cornerstones of every customer–seller partnership. When they are the foundation of a relationship, other benefits accrue around them. The partners can help each other. They can respect each other, motivate each other when the going gets tough, keep each other honest, and play the outfield for each other so that competitors of the partnership find it hard to score points against the partners.

Being a partner in a profit improvement relationship can be taught to your salespeople in this way: Your products and services, plus your personal expertise in applying them, can help your customers improve their profit. They may be able to help cut customer costs and they may help customers earn new revenues by boosting their sales. As a result, you can improve your own profit on sales because you can sell more, or sell more often, or justify a premium price for what you sell. This is what being partners means. It is founded on bringing into harmony three areas of your needs and the needs of your customers:

1. *Shared need revelation,* which allows you and your customer to understand what each of you wants out of a deal.
2. *Shared need adjustment,* which helps you and your customer to give where you can give while you both hold fast where you cannot yield.
3. *Shared need fulfillment,* which brings winning to you and your customer.

Through a partnership approach, profit is positioned as

the keystone objective which you and your customers share in common. Negotiation is positioned as the sales strategy which you will share with your customers in order for both of you to win your common objectives. Negotiation is the language of partners. It is the way partners talk to each other as they strive, each in his own way, to improve their profitability by working together.

12

How to teach
profit improvement
selling

Teaching your salespeople to sell by taking a profit improvement approach to customer problems and opportunities can accelerate their development as profit producers and the achievement of your sales growth objectives.

In order to teach the profit improvement approach to selling, you will have to know four things: (1) what it means to improve customer profit, (2) how to seek out profit improvement opportunities from decreasing customer costs, (3) how to seek out profit improvement opportunities from increasing customer revenues, and (4) how to make a profit improvement proposal.

TEACH WHAT IT MEANS TO IMPROVE CUSTOMER PROFIT

Setting profit objectives is every customer's business. Your salespeople's business is to help improve customer profit through the application of their business capabilities and their ability to supply products and services to meet customer needs.

Your salespeople begin to improve customer profit from the point at which each customer has finished setting his overall profit objectives. They begin where he ends and they offer him the opportunity to profit over and above his own objectives. This is why your salespeople can have unique value: not because they sell products and services but because they can apply these to improve customer profit. The more profitable their help, the more added value they have for him.

There are two major ways open to your salespeople for improving a customer's profit. One is by helping him decrease his operating costs. The other is to help him increase the sales revenues he earns from those of his operations which your products and services can affect. They may be able to offer him a marketing advantage in the form of a more preferred product or service which can command a premium price or increase market acceptance.

1. Profit Improvement Opportunities from Decreasing Customer Costs

Use Figure 12-1 to have your salespeople enter all the specific ways they can think of that your products and services can help improve a customer's profit by decreasing his operating costs. Urge them to consider the contribution they believe can be made to decrease customer costs by reduced equipment or labor costs, lowered maintenance and service costs, less down time, smaller allocation of floor space or other usable space, reduced insurance costs, reduced architectural or construction costs, reduced marketing costs, and other areas of cost reduction. If your salespeople cannot think of ways to help decrease customer costs, you will have to make sure that they learn more about their customer's operations.

Figure 12–1
Profit improvement opportunities from decreasing customer costs.

1. *Reduced Equipment Costs*
   Include need for less equipment even if more expensive per unit.
2. *Reduced Labor Costs*
   Include direct labor wages and fringes and indirect labor wages and fringes for supervision and inspection.
3. *Reduced Maintenance and Service Costs*
   Include costs of replacement parts and consumable materials as well as maintenance labor.
4. *Reduced Down Time*
5. *Reduced Space Allocation*
   Include value of all space restored to productive use by reallocation of customer's processing equipment.
6. *Reduced Insurance Costs*
7. *Reduced Architectural or Construction Costs*
8. *Reduced Marketing Costs*
   Include physical distribution costs and such promotional distribution costs as advertising and sales promotion.

Figure 12–2
Profit improvement opportunities from increasing customer revenues.

1. *Added Operational Flexibility*
   Include all contributions to permit multiple use from a facility at no or low added cost.
2. *Added Manufacturing or Processing Quality*
   Include all contributions to reaching the objective of zero defects that can enable a premium price to be marketed on the basis of superior quality.
3. *Added Volume*
   Include all contributions that increase volume up to a point of diminishing returns from mass production.

2. Profit Improvement Opportunities
from Increasing Customer Revenues

Use Figure 12-2 to have your salespeople enter all the specific ways they can think of that your products and services can help improve a customer's profit by increasing his revenues. Urge them to consider the contribution they believe can be made to improve revenues by added operational flexibility, added manufacturing or processing quality which can help a customer create improved finished goods or output that can command added value in his own markets, added volume of output, or other areas of revenue improvement. If your sales representatives cannot think of ways to help increase customer revenues, you will have to make sure that they learn more about their customer's operations.

TEACH HOW TO MAKE
A PROFIT IMPROVEMENT PROPOSAL

To sell profit improvement, your salespeople's presentations should take the form of *profit improvement proposals*. This will position them as profit improvers in the customer's frame of reference. Instead of saying to the customer, "I'm going to ask you to buy something," a profit improvement proposal says "You have an opportunity to save money or earn some new money." While it is relatively easy for a customer to say, "Thank you, but I really don't want to buy anything today," it is very difficult for any customer to be serious in saying, "No thank you, I'm not interested in saving money or making more."

Each profit improvement proposal will have to meet three characteristics to be successful. One, it will have to be *measurable*. This means that you will have to teach your salespeople to show in numbers how their proposal actually helps improve customer profit. Second, profit improvement proposals have to be *realistic*. They don't have to promise the moon in order to be acceptable. All cost reductions are good from where the customer stands. Similarly, all improvements in profit are also good. Third, profit improvement proposals have to be composed of *honest* suggestions and not gimmicks about how customers can benefit themselves by doing business with you.

Teach your sales representatives to prepare a profit improvement proposal for each major sale. This will take them through four successive steps: (1) an itemization of the incremental investment required by a customer to obtain the products or services your salesperson recommends for him; (2) an itemization of the annual profit improvement contribution which your products or services can make to the customer, either by decreasing his operating costs or by increasing his revenues; (3) an itemization of the next year operating benefits that the customer can expect from the effects of your products or services on his operating cost and revenues; and (4) finally, a calculation of the return on investment the customer can obtain.

A model proposal is shown in Figure 12-3.* Use it as a guide in creating your own format. The proposal format you create should contain the same four successive steps as the model. They appear in the order of their calculation. At an actual presentation to a customer, the fourth part—the promised return on investment—should be given first.

Study the proposal format you come up with until you become comfortable with teaching the information it asks for. The guidelines in Figure 12-4 will tell you how to help your salespeople enter the proper figures for each prospective customer.

Whenever they do not know a specific figure, teach your salespeople to obtain it by taking the proposal with them on a customer call and asking the customer to share in helping improve his profit. If they still cannot learn a figure, teach them to estimate it.

TEACH HOW TO IDENTIFY
PROFIT IMPROVEMENT OPPORTUNITIES

Once you decide to teach your salesforce the approach of improving customer profit, you will be committing yourself

*The remaining figures for this chapter have been placed at the end of the chapter.

to a continual search for ways to improve the profit of the customer operations that your products and services can affect. You will find yourself asking, What costs can we help cut? and How can we help add new revenues?

Profit improvement opportunities are not everywhere. But there are always enough to help you improve your own profit. The problem is not to create them; your customers' business operations do that. The problem is to find them.

There are five proven ways of teaching your salespeople how to identify profit improvement opportunities in a customer's business.

1. *Study the business* as if it were your own. Seek out its needs for lower costs and new revenues from the operations you know the most about. Become a professional student of your customers' businesses. Read their annual reports and press releases. Talk to their suppliers and customers.

2. *Ask questions* of your contacts in customer organizations. Find out first hand where the main cost centers are and which operations contribute the greatest share of cost or inefficiency.

3. *Read and take notes* from articles in the trade press, in the general business press, and in newspapers or newsletters from investment analysts that concern your industry or specific customer companies. Take notes at trade association meetings. Set up an information file on a customer-by-customer basis.

4. *Request information* on your customer industries from your internal company resource people. Add their reports to your customer files.

5. *Learn what other suppliers know* about your customer industries. Talk with supplier marketing, sales, and engineering executives to find out what expert help they can give you or refer you to.

Figure 12-5 shows a comprehensive "laundry list" of profit improvement opportunities that can apply to many businesses. Check off the opportunities that apply to you. Then use Figure 12-6 as a model to work out the full range of opportunities open to your salesforce to improve profit for each customer. Define the customer operations which contain opportunity, the specific nature of the opportunity in terms of its ability to reduce costs or improve revenues, and the products and services your salesforce can provide to deliver an improved profit.

Figure 12–3
Profit improvement proposal format.

Stage 1. Incremental Investment Analysis

1. Cost of proposed equipment	$39,600		
Estimated installation cost	6,000		
Subtotal	$45,600		
Minus initial tax benefit of	3,190		
Total		$42,410	1
2. Disposal value of equipment to be replaced	8,000		
Capital additions required in absence of proposed equipment	6,000		
Minus initial tax benefit for capital additions of	420		
Total		$13,580	2
3. Incremental investment (1 − 2)		$28,830	3

Stage 2. Profit Improvement Analysis
(Annual Contribution)

4. Profit improvement—net decrease in operating costs (from line 27)	$24,952	4
5. Profit improvement—net increase in revenue (from line 31)	$	5
6. Annual profit improvement (lines 4 + 5)	$24,952	6

Stage 3. Next Year Operating Benefits from Proposed Equipment

A. Effect of proposed equipment on operating costs

(COMPUTED ON MACHINE-HOUR BASIS)	PRESENT	PROPOSED	
7. Direct labor (wages plus incentives and bonuses)	$10.50	$3.50	7
8. Indirect labor (supervision, inspectors, helpers)	3.67	1.22	8
9. Fringe benefits (vacations, pensions, insurance, etc.)	2.15	0.72	9
10. Maintenance (ordinary only, parts and labor)	1.18	0.90	10
11. Abrasives, media, compounds, or other consumable supplies	1.32	1.10	11
12. Power	0.56	0.48	12
13. Total (sum of 7 through 12)	$19.38	$7.92	13
14. Estimated machine hours to be operated next year	2,400	3,000	14
15. Partial operating costs next year (13 × 14)	$46,512(A)	$23,760(B)	15
16. Partial operating profit improvement (15A − 15B)		$22,752	16

(COMPUTED ON YEARLY BASIS)	INCREASE	DECREASE	
17. Scrap or damaged work	$	$ 700	17
18. Down time		1,500	18
19. Floor space			19
20. Subcontracting			20
21. Inventory			21
22. Safety			22
23. Flexibility			23

175

Figure 12–3 (continued)

24. Other				24
25. Total	$ (A)	$ 2,200(B)		25
26. Net decrease in operating costs (partial) (25B − 25A)		$ 2,200		26
27. Total effect of proposed equipment on operating costs (16 + 26)		$24,952		27

B. Effect of proposed equipment on revenue

(COMPUTED ON YEARLY BASIS)	INCREASE	DECREASE	
28. From change in quality of products	$	$	28
29. From change in volume of output			29
30. Total	$ (A)	$ (B)	30
31. Net increase in revenue (30A − 30B)		$	31

Stage 4. Analysis of Return on Incremental Investment

32. Incremental investment (line 3)	$28,830	32
33. Annual profit improvement (line 6)	$24,952	33
34. Before-tax return on investment (line 33 ÷ line 32)	86%	34

Figure 12–4
Guidelines to profit improvement proposal.

I. Initial Investment Required
Line 1: *Installed Cost of Proposed Equipment.* Enter the delivered cost of the equipment and an estimate of the installation costs

in the appropriate places. Subtract the initial tax benefit (7 percent of the installed cost). Then enter the total at the right.

Line 2: *Disposal Value of Equipment to Be Replaced.* Equipment currently being used has a resale value, either as used equipment or as scrap. An estimate should be obtained and entered here.

If it will be necessary to rebuild or improve the present equipment next year, enter the total cost of necessary parts, labor, and the rest on the second line.

Subtract the initial tax benefit for any capital additions required. Then enter the total at the right.

Line 3: *Incremental Investment.* Subtract the total of line 2 from the total of line 1 to show the initial net investment.

II. Profit Improvement Contribution

Line 4: Enter the *net decrease in operating costs* from line 27. Such decrease is one of the profit improvement benefits attributed to the effect of proposed equipment on operating costs.

Line 5: Enter the *net effect upon revenue* of proposed equipment.
Line 6: *Annual Profit Improvement* is the combined effect of reduced operating costs and increased revenue for next year.

III. Next-Year Benefits from Proposed Equipment

The main subdivisions of this section of the analysis are self-explanatory. Effect of proposed equipment on operating costs is broken down into two parts. Items of operating cost, lines 7 through 12, are more easily computed on an hourly basis (converting to yearly costs in line 15), while the additional items of operating cost, lines 17 through 24, are most readily figured on a yearly basis.

For the purpose of this analysis, hourly refers to clock hours. In most cases this will be 8, 16, or 24 hours per day depending upon the number of shifts. For each item in lines 17 through 24, an entry may be made in either the decrease or the increase column.

Entries in the decrease column favor the proposed equipment whereas entries under increase favor keeping the present equipment or no equipment. Line 26 is the difference of these totals A and B and shows the net decrease in operating cost.

Line 7: *Direct Labor.* This is the most obvious and usually the easiest element of cost to determine. Include all ordinary payroll costs such as overtime, shift premiums, and bonuses. Total these costs and divide by the number of hours operated for the actual cost per hour.

Figure 12–4 (continued)

Line 8: *Indirect Labor.* Usually computed as a percentage of the direct labor cost.

Use actual cost records, if available. This item includes shop administration, supervision, inspection, and janitorial and custodial services.

Line 9: *Fringe Benefits.* Include social security, pensions, insurance, profit-sharing, and other employee benefits. Typically this item would amount to about 15 percent of the sum of direct and indirect labor. Use actual cost records if possible.

Line 10: *Maintenance.* This is usually the most difficult cost factor to determine.

If accurate records of parts replacement and maintenance labor have been kept, it is a relatively simple matter to translate these costs to an hourly basis. It should be noted that the costs (parts as well as maintenance labor) refer to ordinary maintenance only.

In the event of incomplete records, it may be necessary to check parts purchases against present inventory to determine actual cost of installed parts.

Line 11: *Consumable Supplies.* Use actual cost records.

Line 12: *Power.* Use actual cost records or estimates of fuel power supplies required by customer operations.

Line 13: Find the sum of lines 7 through 12.

Line 14: *Estimated Operating Hours Next Year.* Use customer estimate or make estimate of probable rate of growth or decline in customer industry business one year from now.

Lines 15 and 16: *Partial Costs and Profit Improvement.* These computations will give you partial operating costs and partial operating profit improvement of new equipment.

Line 17: *Scrap or Damaged Work.* An estimate of the annual work spoilage cost should be made.

If the spoilage results in discarding work, take the cost of replacement less scrap value. If the damage can be repaired by rework, take the rework cost. The importance of this item will vary with the condition of the present equipment as well as the nature of the work.

Line 18: *Down Time.* This entry is not concerned with the cost of restoring facilities that have broken down, which is covered under maintenance in line 10, but is concerned with the cost of interrupted production. When a machine is down, labor and overhead continue to accrue even though production is at a standstill. These costs are lost, along with the value that would have been added to the work if the machine had been operating. In other words, if a machine is shut down due to a breakdown, a rate of loss occurs that is greater than normal costs.

Line 19: *Floor Space.* A value should be placed on net floor space released if it can become usable space.

Line 20: *Subcontracting.* The proposed equipment may alter or eliminate subcontracting costs. The difference should be entered here. Include the incidental costs of subcontracting, such as supervision, inspection, transportation, returns, handling, and expediting.

Line 21: *Inventory Costs.* These will undoubtedly change, particularly if the proposed equipment replaces multiple components or if a difference in parts life can be shown. Such costs as storage, handling, record keeping, property taxes, and insurance should be included if possible.

Line 22: *Safety.* If the proposed equipment offers additional safety features, a value should be recorded. For example, it may permit a lower insurance rate on employees.

Line 23: *Flexibility.* Because of some feature, the proposed equipment may offer greater flexibility in work scheduling or increase the range of products handled. Perhaps it will give greater protection at peak loads. If a value can be estimated, it should be recorded here.

Line 24: *Other.* This item is a catch-all for any additional factors that should be considered. It might include a reduction in handling labor, property taxes, or insurance premiums.

Line 25: *Total.* Entries under the increase and decrease columns for lines 17 through 24 should be totaled.

Line 26: *Net Decrease in Operating Cost.* Typically line 26B will be greater in value than line 26A. This difference represents the net decrease in operating cost for lines 17 through 24.

Line 27: *Total Effect on Operating Costs.* The sum of lines 16 and 26 represents the total effect of the proposed equipment on operating costs. As previously explained, line 16 shows the operating

Figure 12–4 (continued)

advantage of items more easily computed on a machine-hour basis while line 26 shows the operating advantage of items more easily shown on a yearly basis.

Line 28: *From Change in Quality of Products.* If the proposed equipment improves the quality of the product, this may result in an increase in sales price or an added sales advantage. A value should be estimated and entered in column A, if possible.

Line 29: *From Change in Volume of Output.* The proposed equipment may expand the output of existing products or may add new output, or both. Estimate the benefit to sales or cost reduction and enter in column A.

Lines 30 and 31: These entries are simple computations giving the annual operating benefits of the proposed equipment.

IV. Return on Investment Analysis

Line 32: *Incremental Investment.* This amount, entered here from line 3, represents the funds required to invest in the proposed equipment. The cost of the proposed equipment plus installation will be partially covered by the disposal of equipment to be replaced. The amount of capital additions required in the absence of proposed equipment is also deducted to arrive at the investment which is incremental to a decision to buy the proposed equipment.

Line 33: *Annual Profit Improvement* (entered from line 6) represents next year's operating benefits which are being offered through acquisition of proposed equipment.

Line 34: *Before-Tax Return on Investment.* Divide line 33 by line 32. In order to compute the after-tax return, the tax rate, debt ratio, and debt cost must be known.

Figure 12–5
Profit improvement opportunity checklist.

From Cutting Customer's Purchase Costs
1. Reduce the number of types of articles in stock.
2. Standardize preferred items.
3. Shop the market for optimal supplier quality, delivery, and cost.

4. Centralize negotiations for major items.

5. Plan ahead to reduce rush procurement.

6. Subject bids and contracts to periodic review.

7. Conduct make-or-buy studies.

8. Speed up invoice processing to avoid discount losses.

9. Inspect incoming shipments to minimize damage from defects.

10. Speed up disposal of slow-moving inventories.

11. Establish most economical production or ordering quantities.

12. Shift burden of carrying inventories to suppliers.

From Cutting Customer's Production Costs

1. Reduce the number of operations.

2. Reduce the cost of one or more operations.

3. Combine two or more operations.

4. Automate operations.

5. Reduce labor.

6. Improve production scheduling.

7. Reduce operating time to speed up production.

8. Reduce insurance costs.

9. Reduce materials consumption.

10. Recycle materials.

11. Substitute less expensive materials or otherwise reformulate product.

12. Reduce raw materials inventory.

13. Reduce parts inventory.

14. Improve controls.

15. Simplify product and package design.

16. Dedicate an entire production line to one product or customer.

From Cutting Customer's Production Down Time

1. Standardize preferred items.

2. Shop the market for optimal supplier quality, delivery, and cost.

3. Plan ahead to reduce rush procurement.

4. Improve plant delivery system.

5. Inspect incoming shipments to minimize damage from defects.

6. Install preventive maintenance program.

7. Improve personnel training.

8. Improve process analysis.

Figure 12–5 (continued)

9. Establish most economical production or ordering points.

10. Correlate forecasting data between marketing and production.

From Cutting Customer's Freight Costs

1. Centralize negotiations for freight haulage.

2. Plan ahead to reduce rush procurement.

3. Prescribe preferred routing.

4. Stage incoming shipments to reduce overtime.

5. Reduce intraplant inventory transfers.

6. Utilize trucks more efficiently or buy trucks instead of renting.

7. Relocate warehouses.

8. Reformulate product or packaging to lighten shipping weights.

9. Reduce handling costs.

10. Reduce insurance costs.

From Cutting Customer's Administrative Overhead

1. Reduce the number of types of articles in stock.

2. Standardize preferred items.

3. Plan ahead to reduce rush procurement.

4. Combine related items on purchase orders.

5. Establish most economical production or ordering points.

6. Shift burden of carrying inventories to suppliers.

7. Control additions of new articles to stock.

8. Take inventory cycle counts when stocks are low.

9. Combine two or more operations.

10. Decrease labor force.

From Maximizing Customer's Working Capital

1. Reduce the number of types of articles in stock.

2. Shop the market for optimal supplier quality, delivery, and cost.

3. Speed up disposal of slow-moving inventories.

4. Establish most economical production or ordering points.

5. Shift burden of carrying inventories to supplier.

6. Control additions of new articles to stock.

7. Correlate forecasting data between marketing and production.

8. Make secured short-term loans of excess cash.

9. Use large-supplier's credit department to obtain optimal bank interest rates.

10. Speed up production.

11. Increase process efficiency to decrease scrap and damaged or unacceptable work.

12. Combine two or more operations.

From Increasing Customer's Sales Revenues

1. Improve effectiveness of sales department.

2. Introduce new sizes, shapes, or materials or new and improved products.

3. Reduce customer returns.

4. Apply creative sales promotion strategies.

5. Speed up production and distribution.

6. Reduce or eliminate unprofitable products, customers, warehouses, or territories.

7. Improve market position "image."

8. Add brand name value.

9. Add customer benefits.

10. Extend product life.

11. Expand into new markets.

12. Increase distribution.

Figure 12-6
Profit improvement opportunity bird-dogger.

CUSTOMER NAME _____

CUSTOMER OPERATIONS CONTAINING OPPORTUNITY TO IMPROVE PROFIT	TYPE AND AMOUNT OF OPPORTUNITY		PRODUCTS AND SERVICES THAT CAN PROVIDE PROFIT IMPROVEMENT
	REDUCE COSTS BY	IMPROVE REVENUES BY	

V
How
to
manage
your
salesforce

13

How to manage according to position descriptions and standards of performance

Before you begin to recruit or develop your salesforce, you should define the key duties currently required of each kind of sales representative and the standards of performance by which you will judge how well these duties are being carried out. These duties and standards should then be set down in the form of position descriptions.

Quite likely, you have inherited a set of position descriptions. If so, it is also likely that they are out of date in terms of changed requirements or the judgments that you yourself will want to apply to the way they are performed. One of your most important tasks is to update your salesforce position descriptions and convert them to fit your own management style. No manager can manage a salesforce according to someone else's position descriptions.

A position description is an implied contract between you and each of your salespeople. It tells them what you expect of them. It permits them to appraise their own fitness for their jobs and it allows you to evaluate them. A position description provides a simple interview guide for you to use in recruitment interviews. It also sets a foundation for your training and development program. In addition, it acts as a fair basis for compensation.

In Figure 13-1 you will be able to examine a major manufacturing company's position description for its field salesmen. It defines eight major responsibilities, the key duties required by each responsibility, and the standard of performance by which each responsibility is evaluated. After studying this model you can begin to put together your own salesforce position descriptions by gathering key information about each sales task from a variety of sources, including questionnaires and personal interviews with salespeople, observations of salespeople doing their jobs, position descriptions prepared by each member of the salesforce, information from other industry suppliers, and interviews with customers.

A position description should have five components:

1. *Performance standards:* Specific, measurable outputs of the position which are in support of your sales growth objectives.
   EXAMPLES: A minimum contribution of $125,000 in profit from sales per year.
   A minimum of one new heavy-user customer gained every six months.
2. *Responsibilities:* Broad assignments which will produce desired results.
   EXAMPLE: Sales administration.
3. *Duties:* Actions required to fulfill each job responsibility.
   EXAMPLES: Sell the most profitable product mixes.
   Develop a territory sales plan.
4. *Authority:* Freedoms granted in order to achieve objectives and produce results.

188

EXAMPLES: Open six small but high growth potential accounts.

Close out all submarginal accounts.

5. *Reservations:* Decision making and operating rights reserved by higher levels of management.

EXAMPLES: May not authorize returns.

May not extend credit.

Standards of performance make evaluation measurable. Without standards you can only *employ* your salespeople; with standards you can *manage* them. This means that you can help each salesman maximize his contribution to your territorial business growth. Standards of performance also help your salespeople manager their five "*selfs*": (1) self-commitment to achieve performance objectives, (2) self-motivation to go all-out to achieve objectives, (3) self-supervision to monitor their own progress and correct their deficiencies, (4) self-actualization to gain fuller rewards from their jobs, and (5) self-development to grow beyond their current achievements.

SET CRITERIA FOR STANDARDS OF PERFORMANCE

Standards of performance for salesforce evaluation should be constructed according to six criteria.

1. The nature of the sales job as defined in each sales representative's position description. This specifies the areas of activity for which standards will have to be developed.
2. The nature of the salesperson required to fulfill the requirements of the position description, as defined in your manpower specification descriptions and recruitment guidelines.
3. The nature of the products and services you sell, which indicate the sales activities that are required.
4. The nature of your markets in terms of such factors as geographic areas to be covered, number and location of key accounts and other customers, and the degree and kind of competition.

5. The nature of your customers' needs in terms of how they buy, the services they require, the nature and complexity of their decision-making process, and the basis for their satisfaction, which indicate the kind, amount, and sophistication of activities that are required.
6. The nature of your sales growth objectives, which will influence the number of established accounts to be sold in depth, the number and kind of new accounts to be developed, and the kind of selling activity to be delivered in each case.

In Figures 13-2, 13-3, and 13-4 you will see a checklist of potential job performance standards dealing with efforts, results on both a quantitative and qualitative basis, and personal characteristics. Use them to help select standards that are appropriate for your salesforce.

ASSIGN VALUES TO STANDARDS OF PERFORMANCE

Once you have selected the standards you will use to evaluate the performance of your salespeople, you will find it helpful to assign a value to each standard. This enables you and your salesforce to place priority in terms of putting forth effort and going all-out for results.

Use Figure 13-5 to put down your standards of performance in their proper priority rank order. Then use Figure 13-6 to combine your standards of performance with the other elements which describe your salespeople's functions into an outline of an eventual position description. Prepare a position description along the lines of this model for every kind of sales position whose performance you will manage.

Figure 13–1
Position description for field salesman.

1. The basic function of this position is to promote sales to customers and prospective customers within the assigned territory, and to maintain and develop satisfied customers for the company through proper handling of and effective cooperation with other company departments in the solution of customer servicing problems involving research, credit, pricing, delivery, and quality in accordance with established company policies and procedures.

2. The major responsibilities of this position are:
   2.1. Selling
   2.2. Customer service
   2.3. Pricing
   2.4. Credit
   2.5. Records and reports
   2.6. Sales estimates
   2.7. Product specifications
   2.8. Expense control

Major Responsibility 1: Selling
The standard of performance for this responsibility is met when sales activities are planned and carried out to result in securing the desired kind and volume of·business in the assigned territory.

Key duties:
   1. Plan long-range and daily sales activities for calling on customers and prospects to promote sales.
   2. Contact customers and prospects personally to determine their requirements as a basis for promoting the sale of company products.
   3. Discuss problems with customers and prospects and recommend use of company products and services to best solve their problems.
   4. Discuss customer manufacturing and marketing specifications as a basis for recommending the most suitable products to meet customer requirements.

Figure 13–1 (continued)

5. Secure new or renewal sales contracts and lease forms covering customer requirements.
6. Counsel with and advise customers in developing and applying methods and techniques for increasing sales of their products and arrange for the provision of information and services supplied by the company to assist in achieving this objective.
7. Request assistance from district and division sales managers and product sales managers in calling on customers and prospects where top executive contact is desirable.
8. Arrange for entertainment of customers when it will facilitate or expedite desired sales.
9. Keep informed of company policies and procedures and new selling programs through periodic district sales meetings, correspondence, instructions, bulletins, and memoranda.
10. Attend meetings and dinners of trade groups and customers for the purpose of strengthening relations with customers and prospects.

Major Responsibility 2: Customer Service
The standard of performance for this responsibility is met when the optimal type and amount of engineering and sales service is provided to customers in solving their problems in ways that result in the development and maintenance of satisfied customers for the company.

Key duties:
1. Counsel and advise customers regarding their problems. In this connection, refer requests for research department service to district sales manager for approval.
2. Keep customers informed of delivery dates of orders and any changes in delivery dates or quantities, as necessary.
3. Investigate quality complaints of customers, prepare accurate complaint form, submit form and product samples to district sales managers for action, and collaborate in the solution of quality problems.
4. Explore continually the possibilities for maintaining and improving customer satisfaction by working closely with customer

management in establishing understanding of customer problems and requirements.

Major Responsibility 3: Pricing

The standard of performance for this responsibility is met when established price policies and procedures are effectively carried out and when sound recommendations are made for the establishment of prices and price practices which will achieve desired profitable sales volume.

Key duties:

1. Prepare requests for cost estimates on new or modified products showing complete specifications for volume, type, packing, and design, and transmit to sales office manager for further processing.
2. Discuss proposed price with customers and secure approval to purchase at that price, or attempt to secure price adjustment through district sales manager.
3. Notify customers of changes in company prices, contracts, and leases or price practices, as necessary.
4. Determine competitive prices and keep district sales manager informed.
5. Recommend to district sales manager desired changes in prices or price practices which will attain desired profitable sales volume.
6. Keep price lists up to date so as to facilitate price quotations to customers and prospects.

Major Responsibility 4: Credit

The standard of performance for this responsibility is met when established company credit policies are effectively carried out and when effective assistance is given to the credit department for determining credit lines of customers by furnishing pertinent financial and operating information on customers and prospects.

Key duties:

1. Keep informed of financial status of customers, including market conditions and management changes which might affect credit

Figure 13–1 (continued)

standing, and keep district sales manager and credit manager informed.

2. Review monthly delinquent list and assist the credit department in collecting past-due accounts.
3. Call on customers with representative of credit department for the purpose of collecting credit information.
4. Cooperate with district credit manager in determining the line of credit to be extended to specific customers.
5. Prior to taking orders, investigate customers and prospects through credit list or arrange for new credit rating.
6. Counsel with and advise customers in solving their business and financial problems in order to assist them in maintaining sound credit status.

Major Responsibility 5: Records and Reports

The standard of performance for this responsibility is met when all required records and reports are accurately and competently prepared within required time limits.

Key duties:

1. Prepare ca'l reports daily, showing all calls made and pertinent information about each customer contacted, and submit them daily to district sales manager.
2. Cooperate with district sales manager and appropriate sales staff personnel in making requested surveys of sales potential, market conditions, and competitive activities in assigned territory.
3. Maintain a current prospect list for assigned territory.
4. Submit accurate expense reports semimonthly to district sales manager.

Major Responsibility 6: Sales Estimates

The standard of performance for this responsibility is met when reliable sales estimates based on future customer requirements are prepared and submitted within prescribed time limits.

Key duties:

1. Discuss with customers their future requirements and prepare individual sales estimates on an ongoing basis.

194

2. Prepare summary of future requirements of customers in assigned territory and transmit to district sales manager.
3. Review sales estimates quarterly, revise as necessary, and submit revisions to district sales manager.
4. Keep informed of general business and market conditions affecting customers' products as a basis for sound development or revision of sales estimates.

Major Responsibility 7: Product Specifications

The standard of performance for this responsibility is met when sound and accurate product specifications are developed to meet customer requirements, and when maximum practical use is made of standard products to minimize manufacturing changes and costs.

Key duties:

1. Keep informed of methods of utilizing standard products and promote their use by customers to minimize company inventories and process changes.
2. Assist customers in preparing sketches and designs of new or modified products. In this connection, secure assistance from art department in submitting sketches for customer approval.

Major Responsibility 8: Expense Control

The standard of performance for this responsibility is met when sound planning of sales activities results in securing desired profitable sales volume of business and maximum service to customers at minimum unrecoverable expense.

Key duties:

1. Invest company money judiciously in travel, telephone, and entertainment to assure maximum return on investment.
2. Make proper use of company facilities and services to insure maximum customer service at minimum expense to company.
3. Plan daily sales calls to insure maximum coverage of assigned territory at minimum cost of money and time.
4. Review customer claims, recommend settlement to district sales manager, and cooperate with customer in settling claims to best satisfaction of customer commensurate with minimum expense to company.

Figure 13–2
Job performance standards checklist (efforts).

1. Quantitative Efforts Standards

Number of orders
Number of calls per man per day
Number of presentations per day
Number of demonstrations per day
Number of hours spent in field per day
Number of hours spent in travel
Number of letters to prospects
Number of telephone calls to prospects
Number of calls on prospects
Number of prospects under active development

2. Qualitative Efforts Standards

Uses sales aids fully
Uses time well
Plans calls in advance
Routes himself with high cost effectiveness
Limits his nonselling activities
Handles objections well
Closes well
Handles complaints well
Follows through satisfactorily
Installs satisfactorily

Figure 13–3
Job performance standards checklist (results).

1. Quantitative Results Standards

a. Sales volume criteria
Sales volume in dollars
Sales volume in units
Sales volume by customer
Sales volume by industry
Sales volume by product line

Sales volume by system
Sales volume to dollar quota
Sales volume to unit quota
Sales volume per order
Sales volume per man-day
Sales volume per month
Average sales volume per call
Percentage of sales to calls
Percentage of repeat sales to new sales

b. Gross profit criteria

Gross profit in dollars
Gross profit per unit
Average gross profit by customer
Gross profit by industry
Gross profit by product line
Gross profit by system
Gross profit per order
Gross profit per man-day
Gross profit per month
Average gross profit per call

c. Direct expense criteria

Direct expense to total
Direct expense per sales dollar
Direct expense by customer
Direct expense by industry
Direct expense by product line
Direct expense by system
Direct expense per call
Direct expense per order
Direct expense as a percentage of gross margin
Direct expense per man-day
Direct expense per month
Direct expense per profit dollar

2. *Qualitative Results Standards*

a. Earns high degree of customer satisfaction and trust
b. Earns high profitable sales volume

Figure 13–4
Job performance standards checklist (personal characteristics).

1. Knowledge Standards
   Product knowledge
   Product application and installation knowledge
   Company policy knowledge
   Customer business knowledge
   Customer need knowledge
   Competitive knowledge
   Industry knowledge
   Salesmanship knowledge
   Basic financial knowledge
   Knowledge of how profits are made

2. Traits and Abilities Standards
   Businesslike personal appearance and conduct
   Leadership
   Personable nature
   Consultative approach
   Intelligence
   Mental and physical health
   Ethical
   Reliability and dependability
   Ability to instill confidence
   Growth potential

Figure 13–5
Priority ordered standards of performance.

1. Efforts standards

   _____

   _____

   _____

   _____

2. Results standards

   _____

   _____

   _____

   _____

3. Personal characteristics
   3.1. Knowledge standards

   _____

   _____

   _____

   _____

   3.2 Traits and abilities standards

   _____

   _____

   _____

   _____

Figure 13–6
Position description.

POSITION _____

Performance standards
1. _____
2. _____
3. _____
4. _____
5. _____

Responsibilities	Duties
1. _____	1. _____
2. _____	2. _____
3. _____	3. _____
4. _____	4. _____
5. _____	5. _____

Authority

Reservations on exercise of authority

14

How to evaluate salesforce performance

Evaluating the performance of your salespeople has one main objective: *to help them improve.* To achieve improvement, your performance evaluations will have to be organized to meet the following six characteristics.

1. You must evaluate *how much* each one has accomplished so you can have a quantitative measure of his performance.
2. You must evaluate *how well* each one has accomplished his performance objectives so you can have a qualitative measure of his performance.
3. You must evaluate *how expensive* it has been for each

one to accomplish his performance objectives so you can have a cost measure of his performance.

4. You must evaluate *how much better* each one has done compared with his objectives so you can measure his proper reward and give him the recognition he deserves.
5. You must evaluate *how much poorer* each one has done compared with his objectives so you can coach and counsel him to improve.
6. You must evaluate *how significantly* each one can improve so you can design a personal performance improvement plan with him that will enable his next evaluation to be better.

To understand the contribution of your salesforce to the achievement of your sales growth objectives, you should adopt an evaluation program that assigns two targets for appraisal and improvement on a regular basis. Target 1 is your total salesforce productivity. Target 2 is each individual's productivity. In both cases, evaluation is the method by which you can achieve your objectives of performance improvement for your salesforce as a whole and your objectives of self-improvement for each individual sales representative.

THE PAC SYSTEM

When it comes to setting performance objectives for evaluation, the soundest system to follow from both a psychological and operational point of view is the one known as PAC:

P stands for making certain that each sales representative *participates* with you in setting his performance objectives and evaluating his achievement.

A stands for making certain that each sales representative *accepts* his performance objectives as achievable and his evaluation as fair.

C stands for making certain that each sales representative is *committed* to achieve his objectives and to follow his personal performance improvement plan.

There are two methods you can use to implement a PAC system. The first method is to invite each salesperson to set his own objectives. Then you can either accept them or adjust them through negotiation if you believe they are too high or too low. The second method is to invite each sales representative to set his objectives and at the same time set your own objectives for him. Compare the two sets of objectives. Through negotiation, create a third set of objectives which both of you can accept with commitment. Be careful you do not automatically assume that your own set of objectives is the only correct one.

HOW TO EVALUATE
TOTAL SALESFORCE PRODUCTIVITY

The productivity of your salesforce depends on two factors. The first is *effectiveness*, which is your evaluation of whether the salespeople are accomplishing the objectives you have set for them with the resources you have allocated for this purpose. If effectiveness is low, it may mean that performance is low, the resources you have allocated are too low, or the objectives you have set are too high.

The second productivity factor is *efficiency*, which is your evaluation of how profitably the salespeople are accomplishing their objectives in terms of the time, money, and effort they are putting into their work. Efficiency is independent of effectiveness. It is possible for your salesforce to be effective in accomplishing objectives but to be inefficient in managing the costs of the accomplishment.

How to Evaluate Salesforce Effectiveness

Effectiveness is usually measured against the objective of sales volume. This may be either the dollar value or the unit value of your sales, or both. Effectiveness may also be measured against share of market. In all cases, the key factor to be appraised is growth compared to a prior period, generally a month ago or the same month a year ago.

1. *How to evaluate effectiveness according to annual sales*

volume objectives. Set a sales revenue objective for your salesforce. This will be a forecast. Use your present sales revenue as a base and apply your growth objectives against it. Then use your forecast to arrive at a standard volume of revenue per sales representative per day, as follows:

$$\frac{\text{Sales revenue objective}}{\text{Number of salespeople}} = \text{target revenue per person}$$

Then use the target revenue per person to arrive at a target revenue per person per day, as follows:

$$\frac{\text{Target revenue per person}}{\text{Number of working days in period}}$$

$$= \text{target revenue per person per day}$$

Use Figure 14-1 to work out a standard target revenue per person per day for your salesforce.

2. *How to evaluate effectiveness according to annual share of market objectives.* Share of market can be used in place of sales volume, or in addition to it, as your effectiveness objective. To set share of market objectives, determine the volume which contributes to your present share. Then apply your sales growth objective against it. Convert the volume figure into a percentage of your total actual market: the sum total of the market's business which is accounted for this year by your own sales combined with the sales of your competitors. Project your desired market shares over the next three years. Use each year's share figure as the basis for evaluating your salesforce performance.

Use Figure 14-1 to work out share of market objectives for your salesforce for this year and for each of the next two years.

How to Evaluate Salesforce Efficiency

Profit is the ultimate test of your capability in sales management. Sales efficiency means achieving the maximum profit with the minimum investment of time, money, and effort.

To evaluate your salesforce efficiency, you must start with your profit objective. Then ask, How much *sales volume*

204

Figure 14–1
Salesforce effectiveness evaluator.

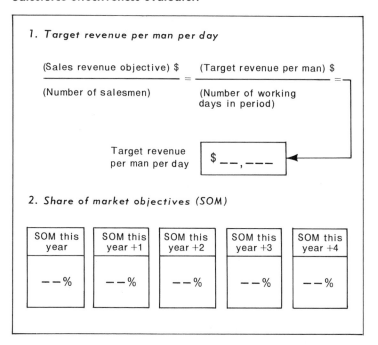

1. *Target revenue per man per day*

$$\frac{\text{(Sales revenue objective) \$}}{\text{(Number of salesmen)}} = \frac{\text{(Target revenue per man) \$}}{\text{(Number of working days in period)}} =$$

Target revenue per man per day $\quad$ \$ __ , ___

2. *Share of market objectives (SOM)*

SOM this year	SOM this year +1	SOM this year +2	SOM this year +3	SOM this year +4
__%	__%	__%	__%	__%

and expenses are required to achieve my profit objective? In this way, you will be acknowledging that your sales objectives support your profit objectives.

There are two basic methods for evaluating the approximate profitability of your salesforce. One is by ratio analysis. The other is an adaptation of return on investment.

1. *How to evaluate efficiency according to monthly ratio analysis.* The most common efficiency ratio is the E/V ratio, which relates expense as a percentage of volume. If you use the E/V ratio, your objective will be to set and maintain a normal expense which will always remain within a certain predetermined percentage of volume. This can help you maintain a standard margin on sales as an efficiency evaluator.

An E/V ratio is a useful guide to efficiency. Do not use it to maximize profit or to indicate a level of sales that can give you optimal profit. Remember, too, that only in

Figure 14–2
Salesforce efficiency evaluator.

1. *Expense/volume ratio*

   E/V Ratio = _____ / _____

2. *Profit/volume ratio*

   P/V Ratio = _____ / _____

3. *Return on sales expenditure ratio (ROSE)*

$$\frac{\text{(Total margin on sales revenue)} \quad \$ \underline{\qquad}}{\text{(Total sales budget)} \qquad\qquad \$} \quad \text{ROSE:}\underline{\qquad}$$

a stable business can you expect expenses to remain a fixed percentage of sales. Expenses as a percentage of revenue must be expected to rise at the outset of a sales growth program. As growth takes effect, expenses as a percentage of revenue will usually decrease. Use Figure 14-2 to work out an E/V ratio for your salesforce.

A second ratio you can use is the P/V ratio, which relates profit to volume. This can tell you how much profit is produced by every dollar of sales revenues. It can also indicate the equivalent volume you will require in order to have an effect on profit that will be equal to a decrease in expenses. For example, if your P/V ratio is 1 to 100, or 100 percent, a reduction of $1 in expense will have the same effect on profit as an additional $100 in volume. Similarly, your P/V ratio can help you learn how much additional volume you require in order to support an increase of each dollar in expenses. Use Figure 14-2 to work out a P/V ratio for your salesforce.

2. *How to evaluate efficiency according to adaptation of return on investment.* A less common efficiency ratio relates

the total margin on sales revenue to the total sales budget. This is a return on sales expenditure ratio (ROSE), an adaptation of return on investment:

$$\frac{\text{Total margin on sales revenue}}{\text{Total sales budget}} = \text{return on sales expenditure}$$

Use Figure 14-2 to work out a return on sales expenditure ratio for your salesforce. Decide whether it is helpful enough to justify making it a continuing evaluator of your selling efficiency.

SALESFORCE PERFORMANCE IMPROVEMENT

The objective of salesforce evaluation is performance improvement. There are three basic ways for improving salesforce performance if your evaluation shows that changes are required: You can improve your sales organization or policies, your market coverage, or your controls.

1. *Improving performance by improving sales organization or policies.* Performance evaluation may reveal that your sales organization is out of harmony with your market's needs. You may want to reorganize the organization by adopting a policy of *systems selling* in which each sales representative sells systems composed of related products and services which can solve comprehensive customer problems. Or you may want to organize your sales along key account lines, assigning *key account salespeople* to specific heavy-user customers. In this way, a sales representative can concentrate on intensively developing the business of a small number of major accounts by learning in depth about their problems and how to solve them.

Other organization and policy improvements include altering the boundaries of your sales territory or industry assignments, increasing the rewards you pay for prospect development, and reviving dormant accounts.

Use Figure 14-3 as a guide to the organization or policy improvements you will make if your evaluation has revealed their need.

Figure 14–3
Sales organization and policy improvement plan.

1. Organization improvements
    1.1. Reorganize salesforce along key account lines.
    1.2. Reorganize territory assignments.
    1.3. Reorganize industry assignments.
    1.4. Other:

    _____

    _____

    _____

2. Policy improvements
    2.1. Adopt policy of systems selling.
    2.2. Increase salesforce attention to prospect development and reward system.
    2.3. Increase salesforce attention to reviving dormant accounts and reward system.
    2.4. Other:

    _____

    _____

    _____

---

2. _Improving performance by improving market coverage._ Performance evaluation may reveal the need to alter your methods of market coverage. One thing it may point up is the desirability of adopting a specialized approach to your key markets. This would require you to designate _industry specialists_ among your salespeople. Each specialist sells to one industry or, at most, to a few major industries. From the point of view of these specialized industries, your industry specialist becomes their chief authority on solving their specialized needs. This is the ultimate step in the market orientation of your salesforce. It also makes systems selling simpler.

Other methods of improving your market coverage include

Figure 14–4
Market coverage improvement plan.

1. Adopt specialized approach to key markets by designating *industry specialists* among salesforce.
2. Improve salesforce utilization of time, by

   2.1. _____

   2.2. _____

   2.3. _____

3. Increase number of scheduled salesforce calls on heavy users per _____ from _____ to _____
4. Improve the use of

   4.1. Advertising, by: _____

   4.2. Publicity, by: _____

   4.3. Sales promotion, by: _____

   4.4. Market research, by: _____

---

better management of the ways in which your salespeople utilize time, increasing the number or duration of their scheduled calls on heavy users, and improving the use of your advertising, publicity, sales promotion, or market research support services.

Use Figure 14-4 to write down the improvements in market coverage you will make if your evaluation has revealed their need.

3. Improving performance by improving your controls. Performance evaluation may reveal the need for a more detailed reporting system from the field as a means of supplying you with better information for evaluating performance. It may also show you the need for increasing field supervision, strengthened coaching and counseling activities, and a redesigned or newly developed training program.

Use Figure 14-5 to write down the improvements you will make in your controls if your evaluation has revealed their need.

Figure 14–5
Controls improvement plan.

1. Institute more detailed sales reporting plan in the information areas of:

   1.1. _____

   1.2. _____

   1.3. _____

   1.4. _____

2. Increase field supervision:

   _____

3. Strengthen coaching and counseling activities in the subject areas of:

   3.1. _____

   3.2. _____

   3.3. _____

   3.4. _____

4. Redesign or develop salesforce training programs in the subject areas of:

   4.1. _____

   4.2. _____

   4.3. _____

   4.4. _____

HOW TO EVALUATE INDIVIDUAL PRODUCTIVITY

Evaluating the productivity of each individual sales representative begins with creating *standards of performance* and then measuring his accomplishments against the standards.

Evaluate Job Performance

Using your standards of performance to guide you, each individual on the salesforce can be evaluated for his performance on the job. Your evaluation will be based on two criteria: (1) How well each person's actual efforts measure up to his standard of efforts, and (2) how well each person's actual results measure up to his standard of results.

Each person's *effectiveness* can be brought out by his performance in the key standard categories of sales volume, expense, and effort, Each one's *efficiency* can be brought out by the E/V ratio of his expenses to volume, or by the P/V ratio which relates his profit contribution to volume. Each one's return on sales expenditure ratio may also be evaluated.

Use Figure 14-6* as a model for evaluating the individual job performance effectiveness and efficiency of each member of your salesforce.

Evaluate Personal Characteristics

Your salespeople can be evaluated for the knowledge, skills, attitudes, and traits that compose their personal characteristics. Use Figure 14-7 as a model for evaluating the personal characteristics of each of your salespeople.

Evaluate Self-Improvement

The objective of individual performance evaluation is individual self-improvement. After standards of performance have been established and each person's actual performance is periodically evaluated against them, your final step in the evaluation process is to work out with each one a specific plan for his personal improvement.

There are two objectives behind each man's self-improvement plan: (1) to help him more fully realize his capabilities and achieve greater self-actualization, and (2) to help him contribute more fully to the business.

---

*The remaining figures for this chapter are at the end of the chapter.

Figures 14-8 and 14-9 show a simple one-two approach to combining evaluation with self-improvement. Figure 14-8 is a monthly sales evaluator for one individual. It spotlights four aspects of a person's monthly performance: his gross profit contribution in dollars, the dollar sales volume and unit sales volume which generated the profit, and his direct expenses compared with total sales. Other criteria of effectiveness and efficiency can be added as desired.

The sales evaluator assays the person's actual performance for the month by comparing it with his quota and with his performance for the same month a year ago, his last month's performance, and his cumulative performance to date for the current year and a year ago.

If any month's performance is below the budgeted quota for the month, specific areas for improvement can be prescribed on Figure 14-9, the next month improvement plan, whose criteria can also be added to as desired. Both forms should be given to each salesperson whose performance requires improvement. His achievement of improved performance can be monitored each month.

Figure 14-10 outlines an annual self-improvement plan. Use it as a model for each sales representative. It is important that the plan be filled out to reflect participative discussion with each of your people. It is also important to note that the plan stresses each one's self-development. This is because no one can develop a man but himself. You must help, but the main responsibility is the man's.

SEPARATING THE "EXCEPTIONAL"
SALES REPRESENTATIVE

When you inherit a salesforce, you will find that the 80-20 rule applies to your staff just as remorselessly as it does to your customer mix and your product line: Up to 80 percent of your profitable sales volume will probably be developed by 20 percent or so of your salesforce. The exceptions to this group—salespeople who compose the 80 percent of your force and who return only 20 percent of your profitable volume—will require initial decisions on your part about their continuity. Should you try to develop them into high producers? Or should you separate them?

Separation is always distasteful. The only way to make it palatable and reasonably free from recrimination is to document your reasoning over at least a three-month period. There are three indicators for separation you should rely on. One is successive monthly performance, which tells you how a person is doing. A second is quarterly improvement, which tells you how fast and how well a person is improving. The third is your gut feel about a person. In spite of what your first two indicators tell you, your intuitive judgment may still urge you to countermand their message and keep him on or let him go.

Your monthly performance evaluator for each sales representative, shown in Figure 14-6, is your best guide to the recent past. It will allow you to make a dispassionate comparison of each person's effectiveness and efficiency. The three criteria for judging his effectiveness are his sales volume, his expenses, and his effort. The three criteria for judging his efficiency are the ratios of his expense to volume, profit contribution to volume, and return on sales expenditure.

Your quarterly personal characteristics evaluator, shown in Figure 14-7, is a good guide to each person's interest and ability in improving his knowledge, improving his application of what he knows, and improving the traits and abilities that can help generate sales. If a man shows significant improvement over a three-month period, it may be wise to evaluate him again in another three months. Has improvement continued? Has it leveled off or backslid? Has it paid off in performance?

When you have made your performance evaluation and examined improvement over a three- to six-month time frame, you should be prepared to come to a decision on whether he represents an acceptable return, either actual or potential, on your investment in him. If he does, you should devote yourself to accelerating his development. If not, you will have to regard him as one of the few exceptions to the highly productive salesforce you want to manage.

Figure 14–6
Monthly performance evaluator.

Sales representative's name _____

Evaluation month/year _____

Product lines and/or services _____

_____

	OBJECTIVES (QUOTAS)	+/− VARIANCES
1. Effectiveness evaluation		
1.1. Sales volume		
1.1.1. Unit sales	_____	_____
1.1.2. Dollar sales	_____	_____
1.2. Expenses	_____	_____
1.3. Effort		
1.3.1.	_____	_____
1.3.2.	_____	_____
1.3.3.	_____	_____
2. Efficiency evaluation		
2.1. E/V ratio	_____	_____
2.2. P/V ratio	_____	_____
2.2. Return on sales expenditure ratio (ROSE)	_____	_____

Figure 14–7
Quarterly personal characteristics evaluator.

Sales representative's name _____

Evaluation quarterly/year _____

Product lines and/or services _____

_____

1. Knowledge application and improvement evaluation

   1.1. Product knowledge   _____

   1.2. Product application and installation
         knowledge   _____

   1.3. Company policy knowledge   _____

   1.4. Customer business knowledge   _____

   1.5. Customer need knowledge   _____

   1.6. Competitive knowledge   _____

   1.7. Industry knowledge   _____

   1.8. Salesmanship knowledge   _____

   1.9. Customer negotiation knowledge   _____

   1.10. Knowledge of how customer's profits
          are made and how to improve them   _____

2. Traits and abilities application and
   improvement evaluation

   2.1. Businesslike personal appearance and
         conduct   _____

   2.2. Leadership style   _____

   2.3. Personable nature   _____

   2.4. Consultative approach   _____

   2.5. Intelligence   _____

   2.6. Mental and physical health   _____

   2.7. Ethical standards   _____

   2.8. Reliability and dependability   _____

   2.9. Confidence instilling   _____

   2.10. Self-motivation   _____

Figure 14-8
Monthly sales evaluator.

Sales representative's name _____

Evaluation month/year _____/19___ _____

Product lines and/or services _____

OBJECTIVES	THIS MONTH QUOTA	THIS MONTH ACTUAL	THIS MONTH LAST YEAR	GAIN/LOSS THIS MONTH VS. LAST YEAR	CUMULATIVE TO DATE THIS YEAR	CUMULATIVE TO DATE LAST YEAR
Gross profit in dollars						
Dollar sales volume						
Unit sales volume						
Direct expense to total sales						

Figure 14–9
Next month improvement plan.

Sales representative's name _____

Improvement month/year _____/19____

Product lines and/or services _____

1. OBJECTIVES	NEXT MONTH QUOTA	NEXT MONTH LAST YEAR	GAIN/LOSS THIS MONTH VS. LAST YEAR	EXTRA EFFORT REQUIRED TO ACHIEVE YEAR'S BUDGET
Gross profit in dollars				
Dollar sales volume				
Unit sales volume				
Direct expense to total sales				
2. STRATEGIES TO ACHIEVE OBJECTIVES				

Figure 14–10
Annual self-improvement plan.

Sales representative's name _____

Improvement year 19__ __

1. Knowledge and knowledge application improvement plan

   _____

   _____

   _____

   _____

   _____

   _____

   _____

2. Traits and abilities application improvement plan

   _____

   _____

   _____

   _____

   _____

   _____

   _____

   _____

   _____

   _____

15

How to support salesforce performance

You can help insure the hit ratio of your salespeople by supplementing their operations with a support system. A minimum support system should be structured from three components: (1) information support, to surround your salespeople's solutions of each customer's business problems with a problem-solving resource team available to every sales representative; (2) presentation support, to increase your salespeople's success in getting new business by providing consultative help to each one in presenting proposals; and (3) case history support, to provide your salespeople with documentation to prove that their promises to solve customer problems are backed by a track record of accomplishment.

INFORMATION SUPPORT

Work with your company's marketing, technical, and financial managers to build sales support teams composed of representatives of each of the three disciplines who will provide close support for every member of the salesforce. Use Figure 15-1 as a model for planning and requesting the support team for each of your salespeople on a situation by situation basis. You will find use for your technical support capabilities when a salesperson requires assistance in proposing to improve the profit of a customer's manufacturing process or when customer R&D, engineering, or new product development is involved. You will call on your financial support capabilities when a salesperson requires assistance in proposing to improve the profit of a customer's financial process and, in all cases, to help prove the customer's return on investment that can result from a promise of profit improvement.

You will be able to use your market information support capabilities when a sales representative requires assistance in proposing to improve the profit of a customer's sales or marketing process. You should prepare yourself and your market research support team member to obtain, interpret, and apply the market information your salespeople will need in two categories: (1) "what" and "how much" customer market information, and (2) "what" and "how much" market information on your customers' customers.

Your salespeople require current and accurate market information about every industry in which they serve heavy-user customers. Their minimum industry information base should be composed of the following four inputs on an estimated this year/actual last year comparative basis: (1) unit sales volume, (2) dollar sales volume, (3) average profit on sales, and (4) average return on investment.

Figure 15-2 shows a model market information profile on which these inputs can be recorded. Figure 15-3 shows a model key account market information profile on which these same inputs can be broken out on an account-by-account basis for every heavy-user customer in each industry. Both profiles should be completed and distributed quarterly to your salesforce.

Figure 15–1
Support team.

Sales representative ————————————————————

Customer name ————————————————————

Customer problem to be solved ————————————————

————————————————————————————————

————————————————————————————————

1. Market information support resource

————————————————————————————————

    Back-up ————————————————————————

2. Technical support resource

————————————————————————————————

    Back-up ————————————————————————

3. Financial support resource

————————————————————————————————

    Back-up ————————————————————————

In addition to knowing their heavy-user customers' market situation, your salespeople will require current and accurate information on their customers' markets: the customers to whom their own customers sell. Their minimum information base should be composed of five inputs on an *estimated this year/actual last year* comparative basis: (1) unit sales volume, (2) dollar sales volume, (3) average profit on sales, (4) average return on investment, and (5) percentage of each of the customer's total sales which each of his own customers contributes.

Figure 15-4 shows a customer's market information profile on which these inputs can be recorded for quarterly distribution to your salesforce.

Figure 15–2
Market information profile.

INDUSTRY: _____

	This Year				
	Est. Total	1st Qtr.	2nd Qtr.	3rd Qtr.	4th Qtr.
1. Unit sales volume	--/--/----	--/--/----	--/--/----	--/--/----	--/--/----
2. Dollar sales volume	--/--/----	--/--/----	--/--/----	--/--/----	--/--/----
3. Average profit on sales (%)	--/--/----	--/--/----	--/--/----	--/--/----	--/--/----
4. Average ROI(%)	---				

	Last Year				
	Total	1st Qtr.	2nd Qtr.	3rd Qtr.	4th Qtr.
1. Unit sales volume	--/--/----	--/--/----	--/--/----	--/--/----	--/--/----
2. Dollar sales volume	--/--/----	--/--/----	--/--/----	--/--/----	--/--/----
3. Average profit on sales (%)	--/--/----	--/--/----	--/--/----	--/--/----	--/--/----
4. Average ROI(%)	---				

You should prepare to support your salespeople in the presentation of their profit improvement proposals in four ways. First, act as an information resource yourself and manage the application of other internal information sources to preparing the proposal. Second, help edit the proposal, paying special attention to its specific promise of the profit improvement benefit. Third, coach trial presentations of the proposal. Fourth, assist when necessary or desirable in the actual presentation.

Before a profit improvement proposal is made, make sure that three preconditions have been met.

1. Has the salesperson accurately diagnosed the customer problem he is proposing to solve or the customer opportunity he is proposing to capitalize on? This means that he and his customer must have reached an agreement on what the problem or opportunity is and that a solution will be valuable to both of them.

2. Has the salesperson developed enough facts on which to base his proposal? This means that he must understand the cause of the customer problem or the source of the opportunity and that he knows which of his products and services should be applied to create the best solution.

3. Has the customer expressed a high degree of interest in learning how the salesperson proposes to help him? This means that the customer must have asked specifically how he can achieve a benefit to solve his problem or capitalize on his opportunity.

The proposal should be regarded as a sampling device. Its purpose is to let the customer sample the salesperson's profit improvement benefit before he buys it. The proposal is also an education tool. It helps a customer learn how to improve his profit. Each proposal must therefore feature the salesperson's promise of profit improvement. It must then outline his prescription of how the added value furnished by improved profit will be delivered and what the value-to-price relationship of this benefit will amount to. This approach focuses customer attention on value, which is something he receives, rather than on the price he must give up. It teaches

Figure 15-3
Key account market information profile.

KEY ACCOUNT _____

		This Year			
	Est. Total	1st Qtr.	2nd Qtr.	3rd Qtr.	4th Qtr.
1. Unit sales volume	--/----/----	--/----/----	--/----/----	--/----/----	--/----/----
2. Dollar sales volume	--/----/----	--/----/----	--/----/----	--/----/----	--/----/----
3. Share of market (%)	--	--	--	--	--
4. Average profit on sales (%)	--				
5. Average return on investment (%)	--				
6. % of our total sales they contribute (participation)	--				

| | | Last Year | | | |
	Total	1st Qtr.	2nd Qtr.	3rd Qtr.	4th Qtr.
1. Unit sales volume	—/—/—	—/—/—	—/—/—/—	—/—/—/—	—/—/—/—
2. Dollar sales volume	—/—/—/—	—/—/—/—	—/—/—/—	—/—/—/—	—/—/—/—
3. Share of market (%)	—	—	—	—	—
4. Average profit on sales (%)	—				
5. Average return on investment (%)	—				
6. % of our total sales they contribute (participation)	—				

Figure 15–4
Customer's market information profile.

INDUSTRY SERVED BY CUSTOMER _____	
OUR CUSTOMER'S NAME: _____	
1. Unit sales volume	__/___/___
2. Dollar sales volume	__/___/___
3. Average profit on sales (%)	__
4. Average return on investment (%)	__
5. % of customer's total sales they contribute (participation)	__

him how his problems can be solved or his opportunities capitalized on in the most cost-effective way. An outline of the five steps in the presentation of a profit improvement proposal is shown in Figure 15-5. Use it as a guide when you consult with your salespeople on their presentations. Each step is outlined in detail below.

Step 1: Diagnose a Customer
Problem or Opportunity

To start off his presentation, your sales representative should immediately answer the unasked question which every customer has in his mind when your representative positions himself as a profit improver: Does this man know my business? If he does, he will know how my business is different from all other businesses by knowing my specific problems and opportunities. Therefore, the first step is to tell your customer something the customer already knows and to show that he knows it too.

What your sales representative should say. In step 1, where your sales representative reveals his personal and

Figure 15-5
Profit improvement presentation outline.

1. *Diagnose a Customer Problem or Opportunity*

   Demonstrate to the customer that you know something about his business that allows you to improve his profit. Based on experience in his business or industry, you know how you can capitalize on a market opportunity by bringing in new sales or how you can solve a marketing, manufacturing, or financial problem by cutting costs.

2. *Promise to Add Value to the Customer's Profit*

   Commit to help improve customer profit by adding a specific number of dollars in new sales revenues to the customer's marketing operations or by subtracting a specific number of dollars of cost from his marketing, manufacturing, or financial operations.

3. *Prescribe a Value-Adding Solution to the Customer's Problem*

   Itemize how you will apply your experience, your expertise, and your products and services to solve the customer's problem or capitalize on his opportunity.

4. *Prove that the Customer's Added Value Exceeds Price*

   Prove that the value you promise to add to your customer's operations exceeds your price by expressing the price as an investment and the customer's value as a return on his investment.

5. *Commit to Manage the Fulfillment of the Promise*

   Control the delivery of your promised added value by periodically monitoring its progress and working closely with your customer's people to help them properly apply your products and services.

---

corporate capability for the first time, he should diagnose a customer problem or opportunity in this way: We know something about your business that will allow you to improve your profit. Based on our experience in your business or industry, we can help you capitalize on a market opportunity by bringing in new sales or help you solve a marketing, manufacturing, or financial problem by cutting costs.

Step 2: Promise to Add Value to the Customer's Profit

Your salesperson's promise to add value to one or more of his customer's key operations is the objective of his profit improvement proposal. The objective is what the customer will buy or not buy. It is what your sales representative will sell or not sell. It must therefore be the focal point around which the remaining three steps in the presentation will revolve. The proposal's prescription tells how the objective will be achieved. The proposal's price will prove that the value of the objective is a bargain. Finally, the proposal's control system will enable each member of your salesforce to monitor his progress in delivering the objective and certifying that his customer's people do their part in making it successful.

What your sales representative should say. In step 2, where your sales representative states his objective, he should promise to deliver it in this way: We can help you improve your profit by X percent or X dollars by adding this percentage or these dollars in new sales revenue to your marketing process and/or by subtracting this percentage or these dollars of cost from your marketing, manufacturing, or financial operations.

The promise of your sales representative's profit improvement objective is the make-or-break step in the presentation process. If his customer says the right thing after he has made his promise, the seller can begin to sell. Otherwise he cannot. Only the customer can open a sale. And the way the customer opens the sale is by asking a one-word question: How?

The question means how can the customer acquire the added value of the profit improvement your sales representative has promised? By asking it, the customer is acknowledging that the proposal's objective seems to meet the three criteria of being a significant improvement, commensurate with risk, and not a threat to the future of his business. This is the key point in the presentation.

**Step 3: Prescribe a Value-adding Solution
to the Customer's Problem**

Your sales representative's prescription is his answer to the customer's need to know how he proposes to achieve the profit improvement objective he has promised. The prescription says, in effect: Here's how I plan to add the value of improved profit to your business. The proposal's prescription will therefore have to be centered around the customer benefits that provide these values.

The benefit values your sales representative can prescribe must come from three sources. The first source is your products or services. The second source is the representative's experience, which he can use to teach his customer how to make the most cost-effective use of your products and services. The third source is the sales representative's expertise in prescribing your products or services and calling on his support services to insure their proper use. His professional expertise, and the experience on which it is based, are most likely to be the two most distinctive components of his presentations. Your ability to price at a premium will largely depend on how well your salespeople can translate their expertise and knowledge into profit improvement benefits that your customers can obtain nowhere else.

What your sales representative should say. In step 3, where your salesperson recommends his prescription, he should introduce it in this way: We will apply our experience and expertise along with the following system of our products and services to solve your problem and/or capitalize on your opportunity.

Your sales representative's prescribed system will then have to be outlined on a benefit-per-component basis. For every component, he should list its economic benefits first and its specifications second. What it is makes no sense at all until the customer knows what it does. Remember that he is selling profit improvement benefits and that his prescription must validate their delivery.

The benefit values of each system your salesman prescribes should be defined in terms of their contribution to either new customer revenues or cost reduction. In this way, their contribution to profit improvement and not just to cost can be justified.

Step 4: Prove That the Customer's
Added Value Exceeds Price

Your sales representative's answer to the customer's question, "How much is the value-adding system you prescribe?" should not be expressed as a price. It should be presented as a benefit value. Your products should be shown to add value to the prescription. So should your services such as teaching, providing information, financing purchase, leasing, and so on. Similarly, your price should also be presented as adding value to the prescription.

The value that price can add is the value of a bargain. A bargain is a transaction whose value exceeds its price. Your sales representative's mission is twofold. He must improve customer profit by maximizing the value he delivers. At the same time, he must improve his own contribution to your profit by maximizing the price he charges.

If your sales representative's prescription of added value does not justify a premium price, help him rewrite it until it does. If you cannot, do not let him propose it. Premium price is the acid test of your confidence in a prescription's benefits. If you do not believe that a prescription can justify a premium price, it is unlikely that the customer will believe it either. Use the model proposal shown in Figure 12-3.

What your sales representative should say. In step 4, where your sales representative defines the degree to which the value of his prescription exceeds its price, he should say: The value we promise to add exceeds the price you promise to pay by X percent or X dollars. To prove it, we express price as an investment and we express value as a rate of return on your investment.

To help your salespeople calculate return on investment, use this simplified formula, where improved profit represents added value and price represents the customer's investment.

$$\frac{\text{Improved profit promised}}{\text{Investment required to achieve it}} = \text{ROI}$$

By expressing value as a return on investment, your salesforce will be positioning the benefits of your products and services in financial terms. This is the language of price. By expressing price as an investment, you will be allowing it to be directly compared against the value it affords.

Step 5: Commit to Manage
the Fulfillment of the Promise

The promise of profit improvement becomes believable to the customer when the sales representative shows how he can prescribe the experience, expertise, and product or service systems to achieve it. His documentation of the prescription's value, along with his proof that it exceeds his price, further increases customer believability. One final strengthening of customer belief must be made. The salesperson's answer to the customer's question, "How can I be sure I'll get it?" should commit him to the personal management of fulfilling his promise.

Management of a profit improvement proposal involves two forms of control. Both are important if the customer is to dare to enter into the implicit partnership which profit improvement selling invites. If your sales representative is going to ask his customer to commit resources to sponsor his prescription, it is only fair that he commit himself to monitor the prescription's progress and to work with the customer's people to make certain it is properly applied. Working closely with customer people must be ongoing if the teaching values that the salesperson offers as contributing to his premium price are to be realized by the customer.

What your sales representative should say. In step 5, where your sales representative commits his personal management skills to insure achieving his proposal's objective, he should say: We will control the delivery of our promised added values to you by periodically monitoring our progress and working closely with your people to help them properly apply our system.

By providing such a control mechanism, your sales representative can inspire the confidence his customer needs to become his partner. Without controls, no true partnership can exist. Controls reduce the risk of surprises, which are the most destructive threat to these customer partnerships. Controls help assure a customer that the sales representative will prescribe only those systems which he can implement. Controls also comfort the customer that the sales representative will be playing on the customer's team with the customer's own people since he will have to work closely with them to monitor their joint progress.

CASE HISTORY SUPPORT

You should prepare yourself to support your salespeople in documenting their claims that the application of their personal expertise plus your products and services can improve customer profit. Case histories are the single best proof of performance. It is therefore essential that you organize a case history portfolio of successful profit improvement applications. Each case history should be composed of the following information:

—The profit improvement that was achieved.
—The customer problem that was solved or the customer opportunity that was capitalized on to achieve the profit improvement.
—The customer operation that was affected.
—Your products or services that were applied to achieve the profit improvement.
—The customer's name and the testifier within the customer organization who can act as a reference.

Figure 15-6 shows a model format for each sales representative to use in organizing the essential facts of his profit improvement applications around the customer problem that was solved or the customer opportunity that was capitalized on. Figure 15-7 shows the same information organized around the customer operation that was affected. Figure 15-8 shows again the same information organized around the products or services that were applied to achieve the profit improvement. All salespeople should be provided with a supply of the three

Figure 15–6
Profit improvement case history (customer problem).

CUSTOMER PROBLEM/OPPORTUNITY _____

PROFIT IMPROVEMENT ACHIEVED		CUSTOMER OPERATION AFFECTED	OUR PRODUCTS OR SERVICES APPLIED	CUSTOMER NAME AND TESTIFIER
$	%			
— —,— — —,— — —	— —			

Figure 15–7
Profit improvement case history (customer operation).

CUSTOMER OPERATION _____

PROFIT IMPROVEMENT ACHIEVED		PROBLEM SOLVED OR OPPORTUNITY CAPITALIZED ON	OUR PRODUCTS OR SERVICES APPLIED	CUSTOMER NAME AND TESTIFIER
$	%			
— —,— — —,— — —	— —			

Figure 15–8
Profit improvement case history (our products or services).

OUR PRODUCTS OR SERVICES APPLIED _____

PROFIT IMPROVEMENT ACHIEVED		PROBLEM SOLVED OR OPPORTUNITY CAPITALIZED ON	CUSTOMER OPERATION AFFECTED	CUSTOMER NAME AND TESTIFIER
$	%			
— —,— — —,— — —	— —			

case history formats so that they can learn from each other how to sell profit improvement on a problem/opportunity basis, on an operations basis, or according to your products or services.

Afterthought

In the preceding chapters we have explored the requirements of your new roles as leader, profit maker, growth planner, manager, trainer, and developer. These are a lot of roles for any one of us to play at all, let alone play professionally. Yet they are the inescapable foundation of sales management: not the superstructure of the fine points, mind you, but simply the basics. This is what makes sales management so tough. It is not just the demand it makes on your ability to step out in front of the troops as their leader. Nor is it just the demands on your business management abilities or your talents as a teacher. It is all of them.

As you apply the disciplines outlined in this book, you

will come to appreciate one additional aspect of the toughness of being a sales manager. How you play your varied roles, and how you allocate your time resources to mix and match them, can be fully as important as how well you put your knowledge to work.

Every day of every week, you will be faced with deciding how much time and emphasis to allot to each discipline. The balancing act you will have to perform can be stated in this way: How can you maintain your long-range objectives to implement all the disciplines while putting out fires in one or more of them at any given time?

Men and women who find an answer to this question are sales managers. Their ticket is not knowledge alone. It is style, the way they use knowledge. In the last analysis, it is your style that will distinguish you as a manager and make the greatest contribution to your success.

When your salesforce evaluates your leadership and when your customers and top management analyze your contribution, they will take into consideration both your knowledge and your style in applying it. What they will lean on and derive greater benefit from is your style.

Fortunately, no book can teach you a style. Your style is your own. It is personal, subjective, individual—the essence of you.

When your style is right and when your knowledge base as represented in this book is sound, you will be able to enjoy the opposite side of the coin that features the toughness of the sales management function. Sales management is a sweet profession. You can do so many good works as a role model for the men and women in your salesforce. This will help them find their own style and, in this way, accelerate their personal and professional growth. And you can improve, tangibly and measurably, the business of your customers and your company. In this way you can accelerate their growth also. In the process, who grows the most? You do.

Index

inventories and circulating capital, 50–51
investment and product life cycle, 103

job enrichment, 34
  plan, 45
  and theory Y management, 37–38
job satisfaction
  defined, 31
  improvement plan, 42

key accounts
  analysis of, 82
  call planning, 84, 85
  market information profile, 224–225
  salespeople for, 207

laissez-faire leader, 9
leader-member relations, 14
leadership
  characteristics, effective vs. ineffective, 10–16
  factors in, 8–9
  myths vs. realities, 11–12
  personal plan, 20
  self-analysis of motivation and demotivation for, 18–19
  self-evaluation, 16–18
legislation, and sales, 97
life cycle, product, 96, 103–104
Likert, Rensis, and production-oriented vs. people-oriented leadership, 10–13
likes and dislikes, and perception, 25–26

maintainers
  and satisfiers, 33–35, 36
  usage inventory, 38–39

maintenance of membership, and leadership, 13
management
  history, and leadership, 12
  leadership factors, 8–9
  product line case history, 68–72
  strategies, 2–3
  systems, 12–13
  theory X and theory Y, 36–37
manager
  orientation of, 15
  role, and perception, 24
market
  coverage improvement plan, 208–209
  information profile, 222–226
  needs, and sales, 97
  position objectives, 115–117
market share, 94
  and salesforce effectiveness, 204
Maslow, A. H., hierarchy of needs, 32, 126
materials availability and sales, 97
McClelland, David C., 126
McGregor, Douglas, and theory X and theory Y management, 36–37
modifications problem solving, 156
money, and problem solving, 158
morale
  characteristics, 36
  defined, 32
  improvement plan, 43–44
  and motivation, 34
motivation
  defined, 31
  and demotivation for leadership self-analysis, 18–19
  and needs hierarchy, 32–33

VEGETABLES, SALADS AND PASTA

MARINATED FIGS WITH WITLOF AND SHIITAKE MUSHROOMS

LUCIO GALLETTO

12 ripe figs

2 witlof (chicory/Belgian endive), outer leaves discarded, base trimmed

50 ml olive oil

splash of red wine vinegar

pinch of sea salt

16 shiitake mushrooms, cut in half

8 slices Italian bread, toasted

2 garlic cloves, peeled

MARINADE

3 tbsp red wine vinegar, plus extra

300 ml (10½ fl oz) olive oil, plus extra

2 garlic cloves, thinly sliced

1 tbsp finely chopped marjoram leaves

1 tbsp finely chopped thyme leaves

SERVES 4

Wash and carefully dry figs, remove stalks and slice in half lengthways.

For marinade, combine vinegar, oil, garlic, marjoram and thyme in a bowl. Whisk to emulsify, add figs, mix gently and set aside for 30 minutes.

Meanwhile, cut witlof into 2-cm (¾-in) slices and place in another bowl. Lightly dress with some oil, vinegar and salt.

Heat 3 tablespoons marinade in a heavy-based frying pan over medium heat. Add mushrooms and quickly sauté for 1–2 minutes. Add figs and cook for 2 minutes. Remove from heat and mix half in with witlof.

Rub one side of each slice of the toasted bread with garlic cloves and brush with a little olive oil. Arrange slices of bread on four plates. Divide witlof mixture between plates, leaving most of the toasted bread in view. Place remaining fig and mushroom mixture on bread. Serve immediately.

DIETITIAN TIP
This could work as an entrée or a light meal; however, to keep the fat content down, watch the addition of olive oil.

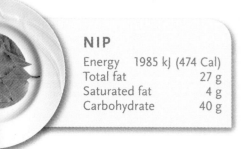

NIP

Energy	1985 kJ (474 Cal)
Total fat	27 g
Saturated fat	4 g
Carbohydrate	40 g

CHAAT PAPRI SALAD

CAROL SELVA RAJAH

I have given you a chaat recipe (cold salad) that is low GI and uses either sugar or sweetener for the dressing. I am using tempeh, which has more protein than the cottage cheese that Indians commonly use. It also has a nuttier flavour and, because we lived in Malaysia, the best cross-cultural flavours and ingredients were used.

My father was a diabetic and lived on dal and brown rice or burghul (bulgur) most of his life. Chaat was his favourite recipe.

100 g (3½ oz) dried chickpeas, soaked in water overnight and drained

120 g (4¼ oz) dried kidney beans, soaked in water overnight and drained

¼ cup (60 g/2¼ oz) dried yellow split peas (chana dal), soaked in water overnight and drained

½ tsp olive oil or rice bran oil plus 1 tbsp for frying

250 g (9 oz) large potatoes

100 g (3½ oz) tempeh or fermented tofu (try Indonesian stores – or use paneer or Indian cottage cheese, but tempeh has a nuttier taste)

1 cup (115 g/4 oz) walnuts, chopped

1 large handful watercress or baby rocket (arugula)

5 cos (romaine) lettuce leaves, shredded, plus extra to serve

2 tbsp boiled or roasted peanuts, chopped

4 spring onions (scallions), thinly sliced

1 red (Spanish) onion, halved and thinly sliced

½ tsp cumin seeds, dry-roasted and roughly ground

2 large green chillies, seeded and chopped

1 tbsp coriander (cilantro) leaves

DRESSING

2 tsp tamarind paste

½ cup (125 ml/4 fl oz) warm water

½ tsp lime juice (optional)

1 tsp sugar or sweetener

sea salt and freshly ground pepper

SERVES 6

For dressing, use a fork to whisk tamarind paste with water. Drain off all dregs and reserve liquid. Add lime juice if you prefer it sour, then mix in sweetener. Add salt and pepper to taste. Refrigerate dressing until needed.

In separate saucepans, boil chickpeas, kidney beans and split peas in water until soft but not mushy. Drain well.

Lightly fry split peas in ½ teaspoon of oil in a frying pan over medium heat for about 3 minutes or until soft.

Boil potatoes until still slightly firm, then peel and cut into 2.5-cm (1-in) cubes.

Lightly fry tempeh in 1 tablespoon olive or rice bran oil in a frying pan over medium heat, then slice into thin pieces.

Combine all the ingredients in a salad bowl and, using a fork, toss to mix. When you're adding dressing to the salad, please balance flavours: if dressing is too sour, add sweetener. Serve with more greens, such as shredded cos lettuce, on top.

DIETITIAN TIP
The legumes make this a great high-fibre meal. Dietitians often recommend using legumes instead of meat, which lowers the fat content and increases the fibre while maintaining the protein content.

NIP

Energy	1701 kJ (407 Cal)
Total fat	23 g
Saturated fat	2 g
Carbohydrate	26 g

LINGUINE IN THE STYLE OF THE FISHERMAN

KEVIN DONOVAN

5 litres (175 fl oz) water

4 tbsp salt

500 g (1 lb 2 oz) good-quality linguine

2 garlic cloves, thinly sliced

2 bird's eye chillies, sliced

⅓ cup (80 ml/2½ fl oz) olive oil

16 Tasmanian black mussels, scrubbed and debearded

1 cup (250 ml/9 fl oz) chicken stock

4 Western Australian scampi, underbelly skeleton removed

16 raw prawns (shrimp), peeled and deveined, with tails left on

16 Tasmanian scallops

sea salt and freshly ground pepper

1 handful flat-leaf (Italian) parsley, chopped

SERVES 4

In a large saucepan, bring water to the boil with salt. Add linguine and cook until al dente.

Meanwhile, in a large deep frying pan, fry garlic and chilli in olive oil over medium heat; do not brown. Add mussels, which will begin to open within minutes. Discard any that do not open. Increase heat to high and add chicken stock. Reduce by half. (The rapid boiling will create an emulsion between the stock and the olive oil, an essential element in the texture of the finished sauce.) Add scampi and cook for 1 minute. Add prawns and cook for 1 minute. Finally, add scallops and cook for 1 minute. Season, but be careful of adding too much salt – mussel juices are very salty.

Drain pasta well but do not rinse. Return to saucepan and pour seafood and sauce over. Add parsley and toss together. Adjust seasoning.

Arrange pasta and seafood with careful carelessness in a large bowl and serve immediately.

DIETITIAN TIP
If you wish to lower the carbohydrate content of the meal, serve this dish with less pasta.

NIP
Energy   3240 kJ (774 Cal)
Total fat   22 g
Saturated fat   4 g
Carbohydrate   91 g

SPAGHETTI WITH TOMATO AND ANCHOVY

TIM PAK POY

Height of summer, just back from the beach, ripe tomatoes, hungry kids; this easy recipe takes about half an hour from start to finish. It suits the busy home cook and is well worth a try. I like to use fresh pasta 'spaghetti alla chitarra' and anchovy stored whole in salt (prawn, or shrimp, is a good replacement but best added right at the end). Toss a salad and, since you have the oven on, crisp a crusty loaf of bread.

3–4 salted anchovies

12 ripe tomatoes

sea salt

dried chilli flakes

1 cup (250 ml/9 fl oz) olive oil

fresh pasta (spaghetti is good for this recipe – allow 125–150 g/4½–5½ oz per person)

flat-leaf (Italian) parsley, chopped

SERVES 4

Preheat oven to 200°C (400°F/Gas 6).

Soak anchovies in water for a few minutes.

Slice tomatoes into two horizontally (I like to trim off the ends as well), then lay 12 halves, cut side up, in a baking dish.

Rinse the anchovies and peel the fillets off, discarding the bones. Dot anchovy pieces roughly over tomatoes in baking dish, season with salt and a little of the chilli flakes. Lay remaining tomato halves on top, cut side down, sandwiching anchovy seasoning. Pour on olive oil and bake in oven for 20 minutes.

Meanwhile, bring a large saucepan of water to the boil and add salt. Three minutes before tomatoes come out of oven, add fresh pasta to boiling water. Remove tomatoes from oven. Place drained pasta on top and dust with parsley. Place dish on table and toss well to emulsify. Serve in bowls and eat immediately.

NOTES: Standard ratio for cooking pasta = 10 g (¼ oz) salt : 100 g (3½ oz) pasta : 4 cups (1 litre/ 35 fl oz) water.

Be sure to store your tomatoes at room temperature (not in the fridge).

If using anchovy fillets in oil, use double quantity.

DIETITIAN TIP
This serve contains the same amount of carbohydrate as almost 7 slices of bread – if you have diabetes or are watching your waistline, choose a smaller serve.

NIP Based on 125 g (4½ oz) pasta per serve and 3 tbsp oil

Energy	2767 kJ (661 Cal)
Total fat	17 g
Saturated fat	3 g
Carbohydrate	100 g

AGNOLOTTI FILLED WITH BAGOSS AND RICOTTA, TOMATO AND TAGGIASCHE OLIVES

ALESSANDRO PAVONI

500 g (1 lb 2 oz) ricotta cheese

300 g (10½ oz) bagoss cheese, grated (see note)

sea salt and freshly ground pepper

8 roma (plum) tomatoes, peeled, seeds removed and chopped

2 tsp extra virgin olive oil, plus extra to serve

2 garlic cloves, finely chopped

250 g (9 oz) taggiasche olives (or other small black olives), pitted and cut into julienne

2 bunches basil, leaves picked and thinly sliced

PASTA

425 g (15 oz) plain (all-purpose) flour

175 g (6 oz) semolina, plus extra for dusting

2 eggs

7 egg yolks

INGREDIENTS OR COMPONENTS FOR 10 PORTIONS

For pasta, place all ingredients in bowl of an electric mixer and mix with a dough hook until mixture forms a ball. Turn out onto a floured bench and knead for about 5–7 minutes, or until dough is elastic and smooth. Wrap in plastic wrap and rest in fridge for 15–20 minutes.

Mix ricotta with bagoss, correct the seasoning and put it in a piping bag.

Divide pasta into four and shape into balls. Take one pasta ball and roll through a pasta machine, moving from the largest setting down to the second smallest setting, taking care to pass the dough through each setting 2–3 times. Repeat with remaining pasta.

Take one sheet of pasta and lay it flat on bench. Pipe filling at 10-cm (4-in) intervals along centre of pasta sheet. Fold pasta in half lengthways and press firmly around filling, making sure you press out all air between filling and pasta sheet. Pour extra semolina onto a small tray. Using a crimping tool, cut out agnolotti 5–10 mm (¼–½-in) from filling. Place agnolotti on semolina and toss gently to dust. Repeat with remaining pasta sheets and filling.

Drop agnolotti in a large saucepan of salted boiling water and cook for 6 minutes.

Meanwhile, sauté tomato with oil and garlic in a frying pan over medium heat, add olives and cook for 2–3 minutes.

Drain pasta and mix it through sauce briefly. Add basil, reserving some to garnish. Serve with reserved basil leaves on top and a drizzle of extra virgin olive oil.

NOTE: Instead of bagoss cheese, you could also use Grana Padano or Parmigiano Reggiano.

DIETITIAN TIP
Alessandro uses very little oil in this recipe, so most of the fat comes from the cheese and olives. If you wish to have a lower fat meal, you could reduce the serving size of these.

NIP	
Energy	2154 kJ (515 Cal)
Total fat	25 g
Saturated fat	11 g
Carbohydrate	47 g

DAIKON AND CARROT SALAD

HIDEO DEKURA

90 g (3¼ oz) daikon (white radish), peeled and cut into julienne or ribbons

60 g (2¼ oz) carrot, peeled and cut into julienne or ribbons

2 small spring onion (scallion) stems, each tied into a knot

1 finger lime, halved

DRESSING

3 tbsp rice vinegar

1 tsp salt-reduced soy sauce

1 tsp caster (superfine) sugar

wasabi paste, as your preference

2 shiso leaves, thinly sliced

few drops sesame oil

SERVES 2

Soak daikon and carrot in water separately. Drain daikon and carrot and place in a salad bowl.

To make dressing, combine all ingredients and mix well.

Just before serving, toss the daikon and carrot with dressing. Divide between two serving bowls and top with spring onion and finger lime.

DIETITIAN TIP
This salad is an excellent accompaniment – tasty and very low fat.

NIP
Energy	174 kJ (42 Cal)
Total fat	0.7 g
Saturated fat	NIL
Carbohydrate	5 g

PASTA E FAGIOLI

PASTA AND BEANS

ROBERTA MUIR

sea salt

100 g (3½ oz) fregola, risoni or other small pasta shapes

⅓ cup (80 ml/2½ fl oz) extra virgin olive oil, plus extra for drizzling

1 red (Spanish) onion, finely chopped

2 garlic cloves, crushed (see notes)

1 tsp sambal oelek or 1 small red chilli, finely chopped (see notes)

400 g (14 oz) cooked cannellini beans (see notes)

1 cup (250 ml/9 fl oz) tomato juice

½ cup (125 ml/4 fl oz) hot water

freshly grated parmesan cheese, to serve

SERVES 4 AS AN ENTRÉE OR 2 AS A HEARTY MAIN

Bring a large pan of water to the boil, add salt, then pasta and cook until just al dente.

Meanwhile, heat olive oil in a saucepan, add onion, garlic and a good pinch of salt and cook over low heat until soft but not coloured. Add sambal oelek or chilli, cannellini beans and tomato juice, stir to combine well, cover and simmer for a few minutes until pasta is ready.

Drain cooked pasta, add to beans. Add hot water and stir well to combine. Bring to the boil, cover, remove from heat and leave to rest for a few minutes.

Serve with grated parmesan and a drizzle of olive oil.

NOTES: This is not a precise recipe – add more or less chilli or garlic to suit your taste. Alter the ratio of pasta to beans if you prefer more of one or the other, and add more or less water to give it a soupier or heartier consistency. Whatever you do, this takes less time to make than it'll take to have a pizza delivered. And … it's even better the next day.

If you use tinned beans, rinse thoroughly and drain before using.

DIETITIAN TIP
We love the way you can add and subtract ingredients to make the style of dish you fancy. Obviously the nutritional analysis will change if you change the proportions of beans and pasta.

NIP	SERVES 2	SERVES 4
Energy	3073 kJ (734 Cal)	1536 kJ (367 Cal)
Total fat	40 g	20 g
Saturated fat	7 g	4 g
Carbohydrate	66 g	33 g

FENNEL, WATERCRESS, PEAR AND PECAN SALAD WITH PROSCIUTTO

BELINDA JEFFERY

This simple dressing is a great favourite of mine and terrific in many other salads too – it's perfect whenever you want a bright lemony flavour. Just one thing to keep in mind: as lemon-pressed oils vary considerably from brand to brand, you will have to taste the dressing and adjust the balance of flavours once you have made it.

DRESSING

¾ cup (185 ml/6 fl oz) lemon-pressed (or regular) extra virgin olive oil

sea salt

⅓ tsp sugar

1½–2 tbsp lemon juice, to taste

small dash balsamic vinegar

SALAD

2 large or 5 baby fennel bulbs, halved and cored

1 very large bunch watercress, washed and broken into sprigs

1 large just-ripe pear, thinly sliced

160 g (5¾ oz) pecans, toasted and coarsely chopped

150 g (5½ oz) marinated goat's cheese, crumbled into small chunks

freshly ground black pepper

12 slices rosy-pink prosciutto

SERVES 6

Make dressing by whisking everything together until salt and sugar have dissolved. Taste and adjust flavours to suit, then store in fridge until you need it.

For salad, slice fennel very, very thinly (if you are fortunate enough to have a mandoline, it is ideal for this). Put fennel slices in a large bowl and toss them with a little dressing to stop them discolouring. Add watercress, pear slices, half the pecans and half the goat's cheese. Pour in remaining dressing (or as much as you like) and use your hands to gently mix everything together.

Sit a small pile of salad on each plate, and scatter remaining pecans and goat's cheese on top. Grind a little black pepper over the lot, sit prosciutto slices alongside, then serve.

DIETITIAN TIP
To lower the fat content of this salad, add less dressing.

NIP

Energy	2678 kJ (640 Cal)
Total fat	58 g
Saturated fat	12 g
Carbohydrate	9 g

BUTTER LETTUCE WITH GOAT'S CHEESE, PEAS AND PRESERVED LEMON

MATT MORAN

⅔ cup (100 g/3½ oz) fresh peas

100 g (3½ oz) broad (fava) beans

2 butter lettuces

2 baby cos (romaine) lettuces

100 g (3½ oz) goat's cheese

200 g (7 oz) preserved lemons

¼ bunch mint, leaves chopped

juice of ½ lemon

2 tbsp lemon oil

sea salt and freshly ground pepper

SERVES 4

Blanch peas and broad beans together in a saucepan of salted boiling water for 2–3 minutes or until tender. Refresh in iced water. Once they are cold, remove and discard shells from broad beans and set aside along with peas.

To prepare lettuces, discard outer leaves, then pick remaining hearts, wash in a large bowl of water, drain, then spin in a salad spinner to remove excess water.

Arrange lettuce leaves in a large serving bowl. Scatter peas and broad beans in and around leaves, crumble goat's cheese over top.

To prepare preserved lemons, cut rind into thin strips and scatter through salad along with chopped mint.

In a separate bowl, mix together lemon juice and lemon oil. Season generously with salt and pepper, taste then spoon over salad and serve.

DIETITIAN TIP
A great high-fibre salad due to the addition of the peas and broad beans – and quite modest in the fat department.

NIP

Energy	974 kJ (233 Cal)
Total fat	15 g
Saturated fat	5 g
Carbohydrate	7 g

10-MINUTE MAGIC PASTA WITH CAULIFLOWER

ANN OLIVER

30 g (1 oz) sea salt

extra virgin olive oil

100 g (3½ oz) French shallot or red (Spanish) onion, fried until golden in extra virgin olive oil

2 large garlic cloves, crushed with the back of a knife and sautéed in a little olive oil, or 20 g (¾ oz) roasted garlic

500 g (1 lb 2 oz) good-quality dried pasta

500 g (1 lb 2 oz) cauliflower, cut into medium-size florets

80 g (2¾ oz) sultanas (golden raisins) or currants

3 handfuls green vegetables (rapini is great but not English spinach as you get a nasty metallic scum)

50 g (1¾ oz) crushed toasted walnuts

sea salt and freshly ground pepper

lots of flat-leaf (Italian) parsley and fennel tops, roughly chopped

SERVES 4

Set a large saucepan of water over high heat and add salt and a splash of olive oil. Put shallot or onion and garlic into a heatproof bowl large enough to easily hold all ingredients and sit it on top of pan. When water boils, remove bowl from top of pan, add pasta to pan, stir and, when water boils again, cook for 5 minutes. Add cauliflower to pan and cook for 4 minutes. Add sultanas, stir for 30 seconds, then add greens, stir through, cook for another 30 seconds and immediately tip into a colander and drain.

Tip pasta and cauliflower mixture into bowl with shallot or onion and garlic, add a good splash of olive oil and the walnuts and toss. Season with salt and pepper and adjust as required. Stir through some parsley and fennel tops and put pasta into a warmed serving bowl. Scatter last of herbs over top and serve immediately.

DIETITIAN TIP
What a great use of cauliflower. This is a hearty serving size, so eat less if you are watching your weight.

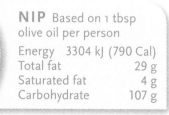

NIP Based on 1 tbsp olive oil per person
Energy   3304 kJ (790 Cal)
Total fat   29 g
Saturated fat   4 g
Carbohydrate   107 g

FIG, MANCHEGO, WALNUT, GRAPE AND ROCKET SALAD

CHRISTOPHER WHITEHEAD

2 figs, halved

40 g (1½ oz) Manchego cheese, sliced

20 g (¾ oz) red grapes, halved and seeds removed

20 g (¾ oz) white grapes, halved and seeds removed

20 g (¾ oz) walnuts, toasted and peeled

large handful rocket (arugula) leaves

1 red radish, sliced

2 tsp preserved lemon, cut into julienne

1 tsp capers, rinsed and blanched

2 tbsp flat-leaf (Italian) parsley leaves

FIG VINAIGRETTE

sea salt

1½ tbsp fig balsamic vinegar

3 tbsp extra virgin olive oil

2 tbsp walnut oil

freshly ground pepper

SERVES 2

For fig vinaigrette, dissolve salt in vinegar. Add rest of ingredients and whisk to combine.

Combine all salad ingredients in a bowl, dress with a little vinaigrette and gently toss. Drizzle a little extra vinaigrette over salad and around plate.

DIETITIAN TIP

The low-carbohydrate content of this recipe means it will have little effect on blood glucose levels, but watch the fat content. If you are watching your weight or cholesterol, one serve is enough fat for nearly a whole day.

NIP

Energy	1721 kJ (411 Cal)
Total fat	38 g
Saturated fat	9 g
Carbohydrate	9 g

SALAD OF WARM MUSHROOMS, BLACK CLOUD-EAR FUNGUS AND PASTA

CHEONG LIEW

30 g (1 oz) dried black cloud-ear fungus, soaked in warm water, hard bits removed and rinsed

6 dried Chinese mushrooms, stems removed, soaked in warm water, squeezed and rinsed

1 cup (250 ml/9 fl oz) rice bran oil, for deep-frying plus 1 tbsp extra

½ Chinese cabbage (wong bok), white stems only, cut into long strips

sea salt

2 French shallots, finely chopped

50 g (1¾ oz) abalone mushrooms, torn

50 g (1¾ oz) shiitake mushrooms, washed and sliced

50 g (1¾ oz) enoki mushrooms, trimmed, washed and separated

1 tbsp light soy sauce

2 tbsp mirin

1 oak leaf lettuce, leaves separated

200 g (7 oz) fresh fine pasta, blanched and refreshed

1 stalk spring onion (scallion), sliced whites only

1 tsp sesame seeds, toasted

MARINADE

1 tsp ginger juice

1 tsp soy sauce

pinch of freshly ground pepper

1 tsp wheat starch

1 tsp rice bran oil

ASIAN DRESSING

½ tsp sesame oil

½ tsp chilli oil

½ tsp oyster sauce

1 tbsp balsamic vinegar

2 tbsp sunflower seed oil

1 tbsp soy sauce

2 tbsp dark soy sauce

1 tbsp mirin

2 drops Chinese rose wine

SERVES 4–6

Put cloud-ear fungus in a saucepan of water over high heat and boil for 3 minutes, drain, rinse in cold water and pat dry. Put Chinese mushrooms in a saucepan of cold water and bring to the boil, simmer for 5 minutes, drain, rinse in cold water and pat dry with paper towel. Cut into slices.

For marinade, combine ginger juice, soy sauce, pepper, wheat starch and rice bran oil in a bowl and marinate Chinese mushrooms for a few minutes.

To cook and seal the cabbage, giving it a smooth, silky texture, heat 1 cup rice bran oil in a wok or large saucepan over medium heat, add cabbage stems a bit at a time and deep-fry till they are wilted and blanched. Strain oil and set aside.

In a dry wok or saucepan over low heat, dry-fry cloud-ear fungus for a few seconds to remove dampness and flavour from the drying process so it can take on fresh flavours of the dish (it will also give the fungus a better texture). Remove from wok and set aside.

Add 1 tablespoon rice bran oil and salt to wok, add shallot and cook for a few seconds. Add sliced Chinese mushrooms and cook until fragrant. Add abalone, shiitake and enoki mushrooms and cloud-ear fungus and stir-fry evenly for only a few seconds. Add light soy sauce and mirin and cook until there is very little liquid.

For Asian dressing, mix together all ingredients.

To serve, toss cooked mushroom mixture and oak leaf lettuce with cold cooked pasta. Add enough Asian dressing for optimum flavours. Garnish with spring onions and sesame seeds.

DIETITIAN TIP
Served as a side dish, entrée or light meal, this is a low-fat choice as long as you are careful with the addition of the dressing.

NIP
Energy	1371 kJ (328 Cal)
Total fat	20 g
Saturated fat	4 g
Carbohydrate	33 g

PENNE DI FARRO INTEGRALE CON RAGU DI VERDURE

WHOLEMEAL SPELT PENNE WITH VEGETABLE RAGU

GEORGE POMPEI

Both my recipes in this book are typically Italian, and rich in complex carbohydrates, legumes and fibre.

300 g (10½ oz) ripe tomatoes

½ bunch basil, leaves picked and chopped

3 tbsp extra virgin olive oil

800 g (1 lb 12 oz) mixed seasonal vegetables (could typically include onion, carrot, celery, peas, zucchini [courgette] and eggplant [aubergine]), cut into small cubes

500 g (1 lb 2 oz) wholemeal spelt penne

freshly grated Parmigiano Reggiano cheese

SERVES 4

To loosen tomato skins, plunge tomatoes into boiling water for 30 seconds. Remove with tongs, peel, then quarter tomatoes, discarding seeds. Dice and place in a bowl. Add basil and set aside.

Warm 2 tablespoons olive oil in a large frying pan over low–medium heat and sauté mixed vegetables until they are soft and just starting to turn golden, about 20 minutes. If needed, add a little hot water to prevent the vegetables from sticking. Add tomato and basil and cook for a further 10 minutes.

Bring a large saucepan of water to the boil and cook penne for 8 minutes, or until al dente. (You could add a little salt to water just as it begins to boil but that may be unnecessary as the dish will be finished with freshly grated Parmigiano Reggiano.) Drain penne, reserving a cup (250 ml/9 fl oz) of cooking water, and add to pan with vegetable ragu. Mix well, adding remaining olive oil and a little reserved cooking water. Serve immediately with some Parmigiano Reggiano.

DIETITIAN TIP
This recipe contains 18 g (¾ oz) fibre. All those vegetables combined with a wholemeal pasta make this just about the highest fibre recipe you'll find in the whole book.

NIP Based on 3 tbsp olive oil and 1 tbsp parmesan

Energy	2699 kJ (645 Cal)
Total fat	19 g
Saturated fat	4 g
Carbohydrate	84 g

BUNDABERG TOMATO SALAD WITH MOZZARELLA AND GRILLED ONION VINAIGRETTE

DAVID PUGH

6 sun-ripened tomatoes, cored and cut into 1-cm (½-in) thick slices

1 large red (Spanish) onion, cut into 5-mm (¼-in) thick slices

4 mozzarella balls (250 g/9 oz), cut into 1-cm (½-in) thick slices

12 marinated anchovy fillets, cut in half

2 tsp baby capers, rinsed and squeezed dry

18 kalamata olives

18 basil leaves

crusty bread, to serve

GRILLED ONION VINAIGRETTE

3 red (Spanish) onions, cut into 2-cm (¾-in) thick slices

⅓ cup (80 ml/2½ fl oz) extra virgin olive oil, plus extra for brushing

sea salt

1 tbsp balsamic vinegar

1 tsp sherry vinegar

freshly ground pepper

SERVES 6

For grilled onion vinaigrette, brush onion slices with olive oil and sprinkle with salt. Either grill (broil) or barbecue on high heat till lightly charred on both sides, 3–4 minutes. Cool and chop finely. In a bowl, mix onion, vinegars and olive oil. Season to taste with salt and pepper.

To assemble, lay alternating pieces of tomato, onion and mozzarella on six plates. Then drape 4 pieces of anchovy on top and follow with a sprinkle of baby capers, 3 olives and 3 basil leaves. Dress with grilled onion vinaigrette and serve with warm crusty bread.

DIETITIAN TIP
Good for a light lunch or dinner served with bread, as David suggests.

NIP
Energy   2192 kJ (524 Cal)
Total fat   40 g
Saturated fat   19 g
Carbohydrate   5 g

SALAD OF POTATO, BLACK CLOUD-EAR FUNGUS AND FRESH HERBS WITH GINGER DRESSING

KYLIE KWONG

2 potatoes, peeled

1 small carrot, peeled

100 g (3½ oz) fresh black cloud-ear fungus, torn into smaller pieces

½ bunch basil, leaves picked

½ bunch mint, leaves picked

½ bunch dill, leaves picked

½ bunch coriander (cilantro), leaves picked

GINGER DRESSING

6-cm (2½-in) piece ginger (35 g/1¼ oz), diced

¼ cup (55 g/2 oz) brown sugar

2½ tbsp organic brown rice vinegar

2½ tbsp organic tamari

½ teaspoon sesame oil

2½ tbsp organic extra virgin olive oil

SERVES 4 AS PART OF A SHARED MEAL

Using a mandoline or very sharp knife, cut potatoes into fine strips. Bring a pan of water to the boil, add potato strips and cook for 4 minutes. Strain, then refresh under cold running water, draining well. Place cooked potato strips in a large bowl.

Using a mandoline or a very sharp knife, cut carrot into fine strips, then add to bowl, along with remaining ingredients.

To make the dressing, use a mortar and pestle to pound ginger and sugar to a paste. Use the pestle to stir in vinegar, tamari and sesame oil, then slowly stir in olive oil.

Pour dressing over salad, mix, then serve.

DIETITIAN TIP
Most of the carbohydrate in this recipe comes from the potato — only a small amount is contributed by the brown sugar in the dressing.

NIP

Energy	978 kJ (234 Cal)
Total fat	12 g
Saturated fat	2 g
Carbohydrate	25 g

SALAD OF FUSILLI WITH EGGPLANT, RICOTTA AND RAW TOMATO

DAMIEN PIGNOLET

A room-temperature pasta salad can be a welcome entrée in hot weather, provided it is kept simple. Tossing the hot pasta with raw tomato, fine olive oil and basil is about as easy as it gets, yet this dish is very satisfying. I recall eating such a salad on a hot summer's night at Armando Percuoco's Pulcinella Restaurant in the early 1980s. Armando cooked the linguine rather al dente and tossed it with tomato full of summer sunshine.

My recipe calls for thin fusilli (meaning 'spring-shaped'), which have the advantage of holding the soft ingredients within their crevices. Personally, I would not serve it as a main course simply because it can be a bit heavy to eat as a large portion.

1 large eggplant (aubergine), cut lengthways into 1-cm (½-in) thick slices

sea salt

⅓ cup (80 ml/2½ fl oz) extra virgin olive oil, plus extra for cooking

400 g (14 oz) fusilli

6 fully ripened tomatoes, roughly cut into 1-cm (½-in) chunks

200 g (7 oz) firm full-cream ricotta cheese, crumbled

1 handful basil leaves, gently torn into small pieces

freshly ground pepper

SERVES 6

Put eggplant in a colander, sprinkle with salt and place a plate on top to compress. Leave to drain for up to 45 minutes, then dry each slice well with paper towel.

Preheat oven to 80°C (175°F/Gas ¼).

Heat a cast-iron chargrill pan or heavy-based frying pan over medium heat and brush eggplant slices lightly with oil. Cook until eggplant is soft and slightly caramelised. Transfer to a plate and use a fork to break each slice into small pieces. Cover and keep warm in oven.

Cook fusilli in a saucepan of salted boiling water for a minute or so less than directed on packet; the pasta should be quite al dente.

Drain fusilli and tip into a large bowl, then add warm eggplant, tomato, ricotta and basil. Anoint with some olive oil and pepper, then toss well; be careful – too much oil will only make the salad heavy. Leave to cool to room temperature, then transfer to a deep platter or salad bowl and serve.

This recipe is from *Salades* by Damien Pignolet (Penguin/Lantern, 2010).

DIETITIAN TIP
Avoid adding too much extra oil to this salad.

NIP

Energy	1785 kJ (427 Cal)
Total fat	17 g
Saturated fat	4 g
Carbohydrate	53 g

PANCETTA, GOAT'S MILK RICOTTA AND SILVERBEET ROTOLO

RODNEY DUNN

2 tbsp olive oil

1 small onion, thinly sliced

2 garlic cloves, finely chopped

1 bunch (about 750 g/1 lb 10 oz) silverbeet (Swiss chard), leaves and stalks separated, stalks finely chopped

750 g (1 lb 10 oz) goat's milk ricotta (see recipe opposite), drained

1 egg, beaten

½ cup (70 g/2½ oz) finely grated parmesan cheese

sea salt and freshly ground pepper

1 quantity pasta dough, rolled (see recipe opposite)

14 slices pancetta or prosciutto

ROSEMARY AND GARLIC BUTTER

150 g (5½ oz) unsalted butter

6 garlic cloves, finely chopped

¼ cup (40 g/1½ oz) pepitas (pumpkin seeds)

1 tbsp finely chopped rosemary leaves

SERVES 6–8

Heat oil in a frying pan, add onion and garlic, then cook over low heat for 5 minutes, or until soft. In the same pan, sauté silverbeet stalks over medium heat for 10–15 minutes, or until softened. Meanwhile, bring a large saucepan of salted water to the boil, add silverbeet leaves and blanch, cool slightly and squeeze to remove excess water. Finely chop silverbeet leaves, add to the pan with the onion and garlic and sauté until tender.

Press ricotta through a fine sieve into a large bowl, then combine with egg and parmesan, and season to taste with salt and pepper.

Lay pasta sheets side by side and trim ends square. Brush long edges with water and overlap slightly. Press edges to form a single piece.

Lay pasta sheet on clean tea towel. Using a spatula, spread ricotta over pasta, leaving a 2-cm (¾-in) border. Lay pancetta or prosciutto over ricotta, then spread with silverbeet mixture. Starting at a long edge, firmly roll tea towel to enclose pasta and filling. Secure both ends of tea towel with kitchen twine, then tie at 5-cm (2-in) intervals.

Bring a fish poacher or a large wide saucepan of salted water to the boil, place rotolo in pan and simmer gently for 20 minutes. Using tongs, carefully remove rotolo from pan and stand on a chopping board for 5 minutes.

Gently unwrap rotolo, trim ends then, using a sharp knife, cut into 5-cm (2-in) thick slices.

For rosemary and garlic butter, heat butter, garlic, pepitas and rosemary in a frying pan till fragrant and pepitas are golden and crisp. Season to taste with salt and pepper.

Place slices of rotolo onto plates, drizzle with rosemary and garlic butter and serve.

GOAT'S MILK RICOTTA

5 litres (175 fl oz) goat's milk (cow's or sheep's milk can also be used)

3 tbsp white vinegar

MAKES ABOUT 1 KG (2 LB 4 OZ)

Heat milk in a large saucepan over low heat until temperature reaches 90–95°C (194–203°F). Quickly stir in vinegar and, using a slotted spoon, remove curds as they rise to the surface. Transfer to a muslin- (cheesecloth-) lined colander to drain. Refrigerate until required.

PASTA DOUGH

2 cups (300 g/10½ oz) plain (all-purpose) flour

2 eggs

2–3 tbsp iced water

MAKES ABOUT 500 G (1 LB 2 OZ)

Place flour in a large bowl. Make a well in the centre, add eggs and water and whisk with a fork to combine, then stir until mixture just comes together. Remove dough from bowl and knead until smooth. Wrap in plastic wrap and refrigerate until required.

Divide pasta dough into four, then, using a pasta machine with rollers at widest setting and working with one piece at a time, feed dough through rollers. Fold dough in half lengthways, then feed through rollers again, continuing until smooth. Reducing settings each time, roll pasta until translucent and 1-mm (1/32-in) thick. Use pasta immediately.

DIETITIAN TIP
The butter makes the saturated fat in this recipe high.

NIP
Based on 8 serves

Energy	2474 kJ (591 Cal)
Total fat	39 g
Saturated fat	20 g
Carbohydrate	32 g

MARINATED BEETROOT, SHANKLISH, LENTIL, APPLE AND MINT SALAD

ANDREW McCONNELL

This is one of the first salads we put on the menu at Cumulus Inc. Its distinctive tanginess comes from shanklish, a hard sheep's milk cheese coated in za'atar and spices that can be purchased in many Middle Eastern grocery stores. If unavailable, substitute a good-quality crumbly feta.

2 beetroot (beets)

3 tbsp olive oil

¼ tsp ground allspice

sea salt and freshly ground white pepper

½ tsp thyme leaves

1 bay leaf

100 g (3½ oz) Puy lentils or tiny blue-green lentils

5 spring onions (scallions), finely chopped

small handful chopped flat-leaf (Italian) parsley

6 mint leaves, shredded

1 tbsp lemon juice

3 tsp extra virgin olive oil

25 g (1 oz) shanklish cheese

4 tbsp fromage blanc (optional)

10 walnut halves, toasted

¼ granny smith apple, peeled and cut into matchsticks

¼ small raw beetroot (beet), peeled and cut into matchsticks

SERVES 4

Preheat oven to 180°C (350°F/Gas 4).

Roast beetroot individually wrapped in foil for about an hour – they need to be soft enough to easily insert a skewer. When cool enough to handle, peel and dice beetroot into 1-cm (½-in) cubes.

Combine olive oil, allspice, a pinch of salt and white pepper to taste, thyme and bay leaf in a bowl, then add beetroot and leave to marinate for at least 1 hour, or overnight.

Put lentils in a saucepan and cover with cold water. Bring to the boil, then drain immediately. Cover lentils with cold water again, bring to a simmer and cook for 15 minutes, or until tender. This method should stop lentils from breaking up. Leave lentils to cool in water before draining.

Toss lentils with spring onion, parsley, mint, lemon juice and extra virgin olive oil. Season with salt and pepper.

To serve, drain beetroot and mix with lentils. Lay lentils and beetroot on a serving platter and top with crumbled shanklish, dollops of fromage blanc, if using, walnuts and matchsticks of apple and raw beetroot.

DIETITIAN TIP
This is quite a high-fibre salad that serves as a great accompaniment to a meal.

NIP
Energy   1153 kJ (276 Cal)
Total fat   17 g
Saturated fat   5 g
Carbohydrate   15 g

POMMES ANNA

TONY BILSON

This classic potato dish was named – according to Julia Child – during the time
of Napoleon III, after one of the Grandes Cocottes of the period. The secret
of the dish is in the use of very thinly sliced potatoes.

1 kg (2 lb 4 oz) desiree potatoes, peeled
and sliced into thin rounds

200 g (7 oz) clarified butter

2 garlic cloves, crushed

3–4 thyme sprigs

sea salt and freshly ground pepper

SERVES 6

Preheat oven to 200°C (400°F/Gas 6).

Wash potato slices in cold water and dry
with paper towel.

Melt butter in a saucepan over low heat,
add garlic and simmer for 2–3 minutes. Pour
half the butter and garlic mixture into a 20-cm
(8-in) round ovenproof dish. Add thyme and
arrange slices of potato in overlapping circles
until dish is filled. Season with salt and pepper.
Pour remaining butter and garlic mixture over
potato, then place in oven for 40 minutes, or until
potatoes are golden on top.

Turn out potato, cut into wedges and serve.

DIETITIAN TIP
Save this one for a special occasion as the fat and
saturated fat contents are high.

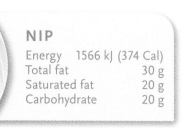

NIP
Energy   1566 kJ (374 Cal)
Total fat   30 g
Saturated fat   20 g
Carbohydrate   20 g

HALOUMI AND CITRUS LENTILS

MAGGIE BEER

juice of 1 orange (about 100 ml/3½ fl oz)

2 limes, 1 very thinly sliced, with each slice cut into small segments, and 1 juiced

6 cups (1.5 litres/52 fl oz) water

220 g (7¾ oz) Puy lentils or tiny blue-green lentils

sea salt and freshly ground pepper

extra virgin olive oil

4 tbsp chopped coriander (cilantro) leaves (optional)

300 g (10½ oz) haloumi, cut lengthways into 12 slices

plain (all-purpose) flour, for dusting

coriander (cilantro) sprigs, to serve

SERVES 4 AS A LUNCHEON DISH

Combine orange and lime juice, then place water and ½ cup (125 ml/4 fl oz) combined citrus juice in a saucepan and bring to the boil. Add lentils, then return to the boil, reduce heat to low and cook for 20–25 minutes, or until al dente. Drain lentils, add 2 tablespoons remaining citrus juice and lime wedges, then season with salt and pepper and drizzle generously with 1 tablespoon olive oil. Leave covered to keep warm.

Make a dressing by combining remaining citrus juice with ½ cup (125 ml/4 fl oz) olive oil, then add chopped coriander, if using, and season to taste with salt and pepper.

Place a frying pan over high heat until hot. Toss haloumi in flour seasoned with salt and pepper, then fry in a little olive oil for about 40 seconds, or until golden, then turn and repeat. Take care not to overcook or it will be too chewy. Remove haloumi from pan and drizzle with a little dressing.

Add remaining dressing to lentils and stir to mix, then divide between four plates. Top each plate with pan-fried haloumi. Scatter with coriander sprigs and serve.

DIETITIAN TIP
If you wish to keep the total fat content lower, use the dressing sparingly.

NIP
Energy	2904 kJ (694 Cal)
Total fat	52 g
Saturated fat	15 g
Carbohydrate	26 g

BRESAOLA, BABY SPINACH, GALA APPLE AND TOASTED ALMOND SALAD WITH AGED BALSAMIC VINEGAR

SEAN CORKERY

200 g (7 oz) thinly sliced bresaola

200 g (7 oz) baby English spinach leaves

50 g (1¾ oz) wild rocket (arugula)

100 g (3½ oz) baby cos (romaine) leaves

50 g (1¾ oz) slivered almonds, toasted

1 gala apple, thinly sliced

juice of ½ lemon

100 ml (3½ fl oz) extra virgin olive oil

pinch of sea salt and freshly ground pepper

drizzle 8-year aged balsamic vinegar

SERVES 4

Toss bresaola, spinach, rocket, baby cos, almonds and apple with lemon juice, olive oil and salt and pepper. Pile up in a bowl and drizzle with aged balsamic vinegar.

DIETITIAN TIP
Despite being a processed meat, bresaola is only 17 per cent fat, much lower than salami. The fat in this dish, once again, comes mostly from the olive oil dressing.

NIP
Energy   1816 kJ (434 Cal)
Total fat   38 g
Saturated fat   7 g
Carbohydrate   6 g

DESSERTS

GRANITAS

JANNI KYRITSIS

Squeeze, freeze, scratch and serve are almost the only instructions you need for granitas.
They can be flavoured with whatever you like and they look great served in a champagne
or martini glass.
There are two ways to make granita: one is to place the juice in the freezer and, as it starts
freezing, scrape often with a fork. This will give you large flakes. The second way is to leave
the granita overnight in the freezer and scrape with a fork the next day.
This will give you small and smoother flakes.

A good guideline is that ½ cup (125 ml/4 fl oz) of liquid will give you 1 serve of granita.

DIETITIAN TIP
What a fantastic dessert –
all of Janni's granitas here
are just like eating a piece
of fruit – just more exciting.
Enjoy!

WATERMELON GRANITA WITH CHOCOLATE

My favourite granita is watermelon. The chocolate gives a wonderful buttery texture to the granita.

1.2 kg (2 lb 10 oz) watermelon flesh
2 tbsp grated dark chocolate

SERVES 8

Squeeze watermelon through a sieve. Pour into a shallow 1–2-litre (35–70-fl oz) container, cover and freeze, scratch (see page 168), place it in glasses and sprinkle some grated dark chocolate on top.

WATERMELON, HONEYDEW MELON AND ROCKMELON GRANITA

400 g (14 oz) watermelon flesh
400 g (14 oz) honeydew melon flesh
1 knob sweet preserved ginger
400 g (14 oz) rockmelon (cantaloupe) flesh
1 tbsp kirsch or to taste

SERVES 8

Squeeze watermelon flesh through a fine sieve. Blend honeydew melon with preserved ginger until very fine. Pass through a fine sieve. Blend rockmelon flesh until fine, add some kirsch to taste. Pass through a fine sieve.

Put purées in three separate 1–2-litre (35–70-fl oz) containers, cover and freeze, scratch (see page 168) and serve in layers.

NIP
Energy	253 kJ (60 Cal)
Total fat	1 g
Saturated fat	0.7 g
Carbohydrate	12 g

NIP
Energy	234 kJ (56 Cal)
Total fat	0.4 g
Saturated fat	0.1 g
Carbohydrate	11 g

PINK GIN GRANITA

½ cup (125 ml/4 fl oz) gin

2 cups (500 ml/17 fl oz) unsweetened apple juice

2½ tbsp strained lime juice

1 tsp Angostura bitters

SERVES 4

Combine gin, apple juice, strained lime juice and Angostura bitters. Pour into a shallow 1–2-litre (35–70-fl oz) container, cover and freeze, scratch (see page 168) and serve.

RASPBERRY GRANITA

2 cups (500 ml/17 fl oz) unsweetened apple juice

500 g (1 lb 2 oz) frozen raspberries or fresh raspberries, frozen overnight

1 cup (250 ml/9 fl oz) water

SERVES 8

Mix apple juice with raspberries. Squeeze raspberries with fingers to break down well. Pass through a juice extractor or fine sieve. Reserve the pips.

Mix pips with water and pass through a sieve or juice extractor. Discard the pips, and combine the liquid with the raspberry and apple juice mixture. Pour into a shallow 1–2-litre (35–70-fl oz) container, cover and freeze, scratch (see page 168) and serve.

NIP

Energy	477 kJ (114 Cal)
Total fat	NIL
Saturated fat	NIL
Carbohydrate	12 g

NIP

Energy	235 kJ (56 Cal)
Total fat	0.2 g
Saturated fat	NIL
Carbohydrate	10 g

POACHED WHITE PEACHES WITH CHAMPAGNE AND VANILLA GRANITA

JANNI KYRITSIS

If you can, use those perfect peaches, the ones ripened on the tree, their skin easily removed with your fingers. The best way to serve them is peeled, sliced in a glass and topped with Champagne. Choose peaches that have red skin as they will give your granita a wonderful pink colour.

I often poach fruit in a freezer bag; the ones you get with the fruit at the greengrocers are perfect. Using the bag helps you to control the amount of liquid so that you don't have any unnecessary liquid left over.

4 large ripe white peaches

2 cups (500 ml/17 fl oz) unsweetened green apple juice

1 vanilla bean, split in half lengthways

1 cup (250 ml/9 fl oz) Champagne (if opening a new bottle, make the granita as late as you can so the rest of your Champagne will be fresh enough to have with your dessert)

SERVES 4

Place peaches in a freezer bag with apple juice and vanilla bean. Place in a saucepan just big enough to fit bag. Fill pan with water to level of peaches. Give the bag a twist so peaches are covered by liquid yet steam can escape from bag. Bring to a simmer and poach until peaches are tender, about 10–15 minutes,

depending on ripeness of peaches. Remove bag from pan (be careful it doesn't split) and place it in fridge to get cold for a few hours before serving (or overnight if you wish).

Drain liquid from peaches – it will make approximately 2 cups (500 ml/17 fl oz) – then mix with Champagne. Scrape all seeds from vanilla bean into mixture, pour into a large shallow 1–2-litre (35–70-fl oz) container (the bigger the surface, the quicker it will make the granita), then cover, freeze and scratch (see page 168).

To serve, remove skin from peaches. Leave them whole or, if you prefer, remove stone carefully with a knife and serve them with granita on the side.

NOTES: You can fill the cavity of each peach with fresh raspberries.

Another simple way of using poached peaches is to slice them, add a punnet of raspberries and turn the poaching liquid into a jelly following the instructions opposite. Pour jelly mixture over the top and let it set.

DIETITIAN TIP
The Champagne gives this recipe extra flavour and only a few extra kilojoules.

NIP

Energy	784 kJ (187 Cal)
Total fat	0.2 g
Saturated fat	NIL
Carbohydrate	32 g

FRUIT JELLIES

JANNI KYRITSIS

As with granitas, I make jellies a lot, using refreshing fruit juices. Simply by using
unsweetened green apple juice with a few slices of fruit or berries, you can have a dessert
on the days you really don't want to spend too much time in the kitchen
(yes, we all have those days).

It is always best to use sheet gelatine as it is a better product. But where do you get it?
I certainly cannot find it in my local supermarket. So I've rediscovered powdered gelatine.
One basic rule is to use 3 teaspoons gelatine to 2 cups (500 ml/17 fl oz) liquid. But this can vary,
depending on how cold your fridge is or how thick you want the jelly.
My advice is experiment to find the right balance.

MANDARIN JELLY

After discussions with the dietitian, I was reassured that artificial sweeteners
are quite safe and easy to use. I have found Equal to be the best when cooking,
so I use it in all my new recipes.

2 tbsp hot water

1 tbsp Equal

1 tsp finely grated mandarin zest

2 cups (500 ml/17 fl oz) strained
mandarin juice

3 tsp powdered gelatine

SERVES 4

In a bowl, mix hot water with Equal and
mandarin zest and leave to steep for 5 minutes.

In a saucepan put ½ cup (125 ml/4 fl oz)
mandarin juice, sprinkle the gelatine on top and
leave to soften for 5 minutes. Add zest mixture
to pan and heat it through just enough so that
gelatine melts (do not let it simmer). Stir in
remaining mandarin juice.

Rinse and drain four ½-cup (125-ml/4-fl oz)
moulds (tea cups or dariole moulds are suitable);
this makes it easier to unmould jelly. Strain jelly
into moulds and refrigerate until set. Unmould
each jelly in centre of each serving plate and
serve with fruit of your choice or with Spiced
orange salad (see page 179).

NOTE: If mandarins aren't available, use oranges,
blood oranges, ruby grapefruit or another citrus fruit
of your choice.

DIETITIAN TIP
What a delicious way to enjoy fruit. Perhaps serve
with some low-fat plain yoghurt or ice cream.

NIP
Energy   271 kJ (65 Cal)
Total fat   NIL
Saturated fat   NIL
Carbohydrate   11 g

POMEGRANATE JELLY
WITH POMEGRANATE GRANITA

When it comes to pomegranates one thinks of paintings before the fruit. European and Australian artists use pomegranates for their inspiration and, of course, Margaret Olley's wonderful painting *Pomegranates* is a perfect example.

I have loved pomegranates since childhood, when we simply cracked the ripe fruit and ate all the seeds from the centre as though they were jewels.

Use very ripe pomegranates. If they are left for a few days and the skin looks a bit dry, they will be even better inside.

If you have the time you can freeze the seeds. After they have thawed, you will get more juice out of them. Place a piece of plastic wrap over them as you squeeze, that way the juice – which stains everything – will not spill. I also use this freezing method for passionfruit and other berries where the juice clings to the seeds.

There is no sweetener required as pomegranate juice has the perfect balance of fruit flavour, acidity and sweetness. The cold granita and smooth jelly create the perfect texture.

12 pomegranates
2 tsp powdered gelatine

SERVES 6

Score pomegranate skin into quarters and break fruit apart. Do not cut through skin and pips as they are bitter. Take out all seeds and squeeze them through a sieve. Depending on their size, you should have about 1.2 litres (43½ fl oz) juice.

For jelly, put 100 ml (3½ fl oz) pomegranate juice in a small saucepan, sprinkle gelatine on juice and after a few minutes gently warm juice to melt gelatine thoroughly. Mix with 2 cups (500 ml/17 fl oz) juice, pass through a sieve and set in six glasses. Place in the fridge to set, about two hours.

For the pomegranate granita, pour the remaining 600 ml (21 fl oz) juice into a shallow 1–2-litre (35–70-fl oz) container, then cover, freeze and scratch (see page 168). Spoon granita on top of jelly and serve.

DIETITIAN TIP
A lovely combination. One serve is equivalent to 1.5 pieces of fruit.

NIP

Energy	595 kJ (142 Cal)
Total fat	0.4 g
Saturated fat	NIL
Carbohydrate	24 g

SPICED ORANGE SALAD

JANNI KYRITSIS

I have made this salad with various citruses – blood orange, mandarin, tangelo
and grapefruit. But above all, it is a refreshing dish on its own. It's great to add fresh
pistachio nuts. This orange salad originated in Moroccan cooking and is best with
ras el hanout (meaning 'top of the shop'). But I have also served it with a
simple sprinkling of cinnamon, which works well too.

12 oranges

1 tsp finely grated orange zest

a few drops of orange flower water, to taste
(optional)

3 small candied clementines, cut into thin
segments, or 3 tbsp candied citrus fruits,
cut into small dice

6 dates, stoned and cut into matchsticks
(coated in sugar, optional)

6 mint leaves, thinly sliced

12 pistachio nuts, dry or fresh, shelled
and thinly sliced

ground cinnamon or ras el hanout (see
following recipe), for sprinkling

SERVES 6

Cut all skin away from oranges to reveal
flesh. With a sharp knife, remove
segments, making sure there is not any
membrane attached to them. Place in a
bowl and squeeze leftover pulp in your
hand to extract juice over segments. Add
zest and orange flower water, if using.

Place orange segments and some juice
on serving plates. Arrange clementines
or candied citrus fruit, dates, mint and
pistachio nuts over them and sprinkle with
cinnamon or ras el hanout.

RAS EL HANOUT

1 tbsp green cardamom pods (3 tsp ground
cardamom)

1 large cinnamon stick (3 tsp ground cinnamon)

1 small nutmeg (1½ tsp freshly grated nutmeg)

1 tsp cloves (¾ tsp ground cloves)

2 tsp white peppercorns (3 tsp freshly ground
white pepper)

2 tsp black peppercorns (3 tsp freshly ground
black pepper)

1 tsp ground cayenne pepper

MAKES 3½ TBSP

Remove seeds from cardamom pods; discard
pods. Crumble cinnamon stick. Chop nutmeg
into small pieces. Combine all spices and grind.
Pass through a fine sieve and re-grind anything
that hasn't passed through sieve. Store any
leftover ras el hanout in an airtight container.
Spices keep for a long time but they are lovely
and fresh for only about a week.

DIETITIAN TIP
Who would have
thought – 7 g (⅛ oz)
fibre per serve. An
easy way to increase
the fibre in your diet.

NIP
Energy   550 kJ (131 Cal)
Total fat   1 g
Saturated fat   0.1 g
Carbohydrate   28 g

BAKED STRAWBERRIES WITH LEMON RICOTTA

JANNI KYRITSIS

Baking strawberries brings out their flavour and their sweetness. If you can find perfect strawberries, don't bother baking them – just eat them fresh. I use apple juice when poaching fruit, as I find it takes on the flavour of the fruit being poached.

500 g (1 lb 2 oz) strawberries, hulled

½ cup (125 ml/4 fl oz) unsweetened apple juice

LEMON RICOTTA

4 cups (1 litre/35 fl oz) milk

1 tbsp lemon juice

SERVES 4

For lemon ricotta, simply place milk in a saucepan, stir in lemon juice and heat over low heat until it almost comes to the boil. It should take about 30–60 minutes, depending on heat. Remove from stove and allow to cool, about 1–2 hours. Strain through a fine muslin- (cheesecloth-) lined sieve for 30 minutes.

Preheat oven to 250°C (500°F/Gas 9). Line an ovenproof dish with baking paper. Make sure the dish you are using is large enough – if you cramp strawberries, they will turn into a stew.

Leave small and medium strawberries whole and cut large ones in half. Place strawberries in prepared dish and pour apple juice over them. Bake in oven for 10–15 minutes. Serve immediately with juices on top and a spoonful of lemon ricotta.

NOTES: I often divide the ricotta into four small pieces and place on muslin, twist them into balls and let them drain an extra hour. When unwrapped, they look attractive.

I find this simple lemon ricotta is a far better product but if you have to use a commercial one, make sure it is as fresh as possible. Or you can use a spoonful of your favourite plain yoghurt.

The whey left behind from the ricotta can be stored in the fridge. It makes a refreshing and nutritious drink.

DIETITIAN TIP

Enjoy this low-fat and low-carbohydrate dessert. For the analysis we are assuming 50 g (1¾ oz) of fresh lemon ricotta per person.

NIP

Energy	489 kJ (117 Cal)
Total fat	7 g
Saturated fat	4 g
Carbohydrate	9 g

SIMPLE RASPBERRY PUDDING

JANNI KYRITSIS

Summer pudding is one of the best English dessert recipes. Like every other chef I know,
I've made variations of the original recipe, using brioche, cake, sponge fingers and so on.
In the end I came to realise that the original recipe using plain white bread is the best.
Cake can create a grainy texture and also adds flavours that distract from
the cleanness of the berries.

½ cup (125 ml/4 fl oz) water

1 tsp finely grated lemon zest

4 tbsp Equal, or to taste

500 g (1 lb 2 oz) raspberries

⅓ square loaf white bread, unsliced

vanilla ice cream, thin (pouring) cream
or plain low-fat yoghurt, to serve

SERVES 6

In a saucepan, bring water, lemon zest and Equal to a simmer, add raspberries and bring to a simmer again, stirring gently to avoid breaking raspberries too much. Set aside to cool.

Remove crust from loaf and slice it into 8 thin slices. Choose a rectangular cake tin or any other container that will just hold two slices of bread. Line tin with plastic wrap, allowing it to overhang sides. Place 2 slices of bread in bottom, spoon on a third of the raspberries, repeat layers, finishing with a layer of bread and some liquid still in pan. Pour liquid over top layer of bread; cover top of pudding with overhanging plastic wrap and refrigerate for 24 hours. The juices should penetrate the bread and no white specks should be seen.

Unmould pudding onto a tray, then cut into 6 slices and serve on plates with the juices. Thin (pouring) cream or vanilla ice cream makes a delicious accompaniment. But a spoonful of yoghurt is also perfect.

DIETITIAN TIP
Raspberries are very high in fibre, so no concerns about the white bread.

NIP Based on 180 g (6 ½ oz)
bread, crust removed

Energy	524 kJ (125 Cal)
Total fat	1 g
Saturated fat	0.2 g
Carbohydrate	21 g

ROSE GERANIUM JUNKET
WITH RASPBERRIES

JANNI KYRITSIS

Rose geranium, and indeed any other scented geranium like lemon or apple, is commonly used in Greek desserts. A lot of the syrups and custard-based desserts are flavoured with a variety of perfumed leaves, sometimes instead of a vanilla bean.

4 rose geranium leaves (or more if small)

3 tbsp water

Equal, to taste

4 cups (1 litre/35 fl oz) milk

4 junket tablets

300 g (10½ oz) raspberries

icing (confectioners') sugar, for dusting (optional)

SERVES 6

Place geranium leaves and 1 tablespoon water in a small saucepan and bring to a simmer. Remove from heat, add sweetener and set aside to cool. Add milk and warm to blood temperature.

Pulverise junket tablets still in their packets with a rolling pin or hammer. Cut tablet packets in half with scissors, empty contents into a bowl with remaining water, stir with your finger, making sure to dissolve junket well.

Remove geranium leaves from warm milk, stir in junket/water mixture, divide between six cups. Let them set at room temperature before you put them in fridge to chill. Place some raspberries on top and dust with a fine coating of icing sugar, if using.

NOTES: For an even lighter junket, use skim milk instead of full cream.

If you cannot get hold of geranium leaves, then 1 teaspoon natural vanilla extract is a very good substitute.

Use any other berries or fruit of your choice.

The recipe for junket on the packet calls for 2 tablets per 1 litre milk but I prefer it set more firmly.

DIETITIAN TIP
You could lower the fat by using reduced-fat milk. Of course the texture will be a little different, but still yum.

NIP

Energy	974 kJ (233 Cal)
Total fat	12 g
Saturated fat	7 g
Carbohydrate	20 g

PASSIONFRUIT FLUMMERY

JANNI KYRITSIS

Here is a dessert that has disappeared from domestic kitchens. It was probably one of those quick and easy recipes printed on the packets of gelatine in the '60s and '70s that put everybody off forever. But a perfectly made flummery is a delicious and refreshing dessert. I have adapted one of my old recipes to suit my needs for today.

1 cup (250 ml/9 fl oz) water

100 ml (3½ fl oz) passionfruit pulp (about 6 passionfruit)

2 tsp powdered gelatine

300 ml (10½ fl oz) white wine

2 extra large eggs

3 tbsp Equal

3 tbsp thickened (whipping) cream, whipped (optional)

SAUCE

1 tbsp water

1 tbsp Equal

2 tbsp passionfruit pulp (about 3 passionfruit)

SERVES 4

In a small saucepan, mix water and passionfruit pulp, rain gelatine on top and allow a few minutes for gelatine to soften. Warm mixture over low heat until gelatine is thoroughly melted (do not bring to the boil). Strain through a sieve into a bowl; reserve passionfruit pips. Cover and place mixture in fridge to get very cold and become firm.

Place passionfruit pips back in pan, then whisk in wine and bring to the boil.

Whisk eggs and Equal in another saucepan for a minute, then whisk in hot wine mixture and put mixture over low heat, stirring constantly to make a light custard (do not bring it anywhere near the boil or mixture will curdle). Remove from heat and keep on stirring until it cools a little. Strain into a bowl, discard pips. Place custard in fridge to get very cold and set.

Whisk gelatine mixture vigorously with electric beaters for a minute or two to break up any gelatine particles and add volume with as much air as possible. Fold in wine custard, then whisk over a bowl of ice until frothy and slightly thickened. Place in four martini glasses or any suitable moulds of your choice. Refrigerate until set.

For sauce, in a saucepan, bring water and Equal to a simmer. Remove from heat, stir in fruit pulp and strain sauce into a bowl. Discard pips. Chill in fridge until set, about 4–5 hours.

To serve, place sauce on top of flummeries and add a small quenelle of whipped cream. If cream is not your choice, flummery is delicious on its own. If you want to indulge, add a crisp light biscuit of your choice.

DIETITIAN TIP
To lower the fat content, just pass on the cream.

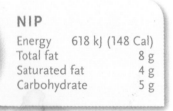

NIP

Energy	618 kJ (148 Cal)
Total fat	8 g
Saturated fat	4 g
Carbohydrate	5 g

GREEK RICE PUDDING

JANNI KYRITSIS

Rizogalo is one of the lightest and simplest of all rice puddings. It is a standard dessert in every Greek household. I have made it for years whenever I feel like a bit of Mum's cooking. I used to make it with 3 tablespoons of sugar and 3 tablespoons of arborio rice, which is best for absorbing the milk and making it fluffy and creamy.

¾ cup (185 ml/6 fl oz) water

3 tbsp basmati rice

pinch of sea salt

2 cups (500 ml/17 fl oz) milk, plus
1 tbsp extra

Equal, to taste

1 tsp natural vanilla extract

1 tbsp cornflour (cornstarch) or rice flour

ground cinnamon

SERVES 4

Bring water to the boil in a saucepan, sprinkle in rice and salt, cover and simmer very gently for approximately 30 minutes until most water is absorbed. Add milk, sweetener, vanilla or any other flavours you choose and simmer for 20 minutes.

Mix cornflour with extra tablespoon of milk and add to pan. Simmer gently while stirring until it thickens, about 6 minutes.

Place in serving bowls and sprinkle with some cinnamon. Serve at room temperature or cold.

NOTES: This basic recipe is lovely on its own but you can change it if you wish. Here are a few ideas.

For an even lighter rizogalo, use full-cream milk with skim milk.

For a richer rizogalo, replace water with milk. Add 1 egg yolk when it comes off the stove.

When rizogalo is cool, add 2½ tablespoons whipped cream.

Add 1 tablespoon finely chopped citron or other candied citrus peel.

Top it with some chopped walnuts mixed with the cinnamon.

Add a small vanilla bean split lengthways instead of the extract, or 2 rose geranium leaves, or a strip of lemon or orange peel, or a small piece of cinnamon stick with the milk.

Since the flavour of basmati rice is associated with Asian cooking, spices such as star anise or cardamom will give another dimension to the dish.

DIETITIAN TIP
Once again, note the difference resulting from using a reduced-fat milk.

NIP	WITH FULL-CREAM MILK	WITH SKIM MILK
Energy	622 kJ (149 Cal)	425 kJ (102 Cal)
Total fat	6 g	0.20 g
Saturated fat	4 g	0.15 g
Carbohydrate	18 g	19 g

DARK CHOCOLATE MOUSSE WITH ORANGE

JANNI KYRITSIS

The first chocolate mousse I ever made, from Elizabeth David's *French Country Cooking*, remains my favourite memory. It was the lightest and simplest of all chocolate mousse recipes and I thought it was heaven. I have made many and various ones since then – some with only egg yolks, some with heavy sugar syrups and 45 per cent cream – but the memory of my first is always the best. In this recipe I have added some orange flavour and omitted the cream and sugar.

In my professional career, I always used the best chocolate. But now my supplier is the local supermarket, I use Nestlé Plaistowe 70 per cent cocoa cooking chocolate and get excellent results. I have also made this recipe with 85 per cent cocoa Lindt chocolate but I had to add some artificial sweetener dissolved with the chocolate/orange mixture.

125 g (4½ oz) dark chocolate (70 per cent cocoa solids), broken into pieces

finely grated zest of 1 orange

2 tbsp orange juice

4 extra large eggs (67 g/2½ oz each), at room temperature, separated

SERVES 6

Combine chocolate pieces and orange zest and juice in a heatproof bowl. Place bowl on top of a saucepan of simmering water and turn off heat. Let chocolate melt undisturbed for about 10 minutes.

Whisk egg whites to very soft peaks. In a separate bowl, whisk egg yolks for a moment and fold them into chocolate and orange mixture. Fold egg whites into mixture and stop folding as soon as egg white is incorporated. Place in six glasses or cups and refrigerate until cold, about a couple of hours.

NOTES: For a rich chocolate mousse, you can add 1 cup (250 ml/9 fl oz) whipped cream.

Instead of the orange flavour, you can try adding 1 tablespoon water plus 1 tablespoon coffee, rum, orange liqueur, brandy, Poire William, or spices such as cinnamon or chilli.

DIETITIAN TIP
The carbohydrate content remains modest because, of all the chocolates, dark chocolate contains the least sugar.

NIP
Energy	673 kJ (161 Cal)
Total fat	9 g
Saturated fat	5 g
Carbohydrate	14 g

APPLE AND SULTANA CAKE WITH CINNAMON CRÈME ANGLAISE

JANNI KYRITSIS

Andrew McConnell is a Melbourne chef I admire. His thousand-layer apple cake is one of the best recipes I know. I've made it a few times with great success and have adapted this recipe to meet my needs today. I removed the sugar and butter and replaced them with macerated sultanas. The sultanas give a dark brown colour to the cake and a taste that resembles caramel. In the end this cake does not resemble Andrew's in flavour but the idea and the technique are certainly his.

Unless your cutting skills are as good as a Japanese chef, you will need a mandoline to slice the apples as thinly as possible.

One good trick with baking paper is to wet and squeeze it very hard to remove the excess water. That way the paper becomes very pliable and easy to work with.

½ cup (85 g/3 oz) sultanas (golden raisins)

100 ml (3½ fl oz) water

1 tbsp brandy

1 kg (2 lb 4 oz) green apples (6 medium)

SEASONING MIXTURE

1½ tbsp brandy

1½ tbsp lemon juice

zest of ½ lemon

¼ tsp ground cinnamon

1 tsp natural vanilla extract

6 tbsp Equal, or to taste

CRÈME ANGLAISE

1 cup (250 ml/9 fl oz) skim or full-cream milk

¼ cinnamon stick, crushed

3 egg yolks

1 tbsp Equal

SERVES 6

Macerate sultanas in a bowl with water and brandy for 24 hours. It takes that long for sultanas to absorb water and become plump. Strain sultanas, reserving liquid.

Preheat oven to 180°C (350°F/Gas 4) (160°C/315°F fan forced). Line a 20-cm (8-in) round cake tin or a large soufflé dish with a square piece of baking paper. Place sultanas in it – they should just cover bottom of tin or dish. Combine leftover liquid in bowl with seasoning mixture ingredients and mix well.

Peel, cut in half and core one apple at a time, then slice apple as thinly as possible. Place slices in a bowl and mix with one-sixth of the seasoning mixture. Arrange apple slices neatly on top of sultanas so you don't have too many air pockets. Repeat with remaining apples and seasoning mixture.

Fold baking paper on top of apples, pat them down well to ensure they are compact and there is a flat surface on top. Cover tin with foil and make a hole on top the size of a finger so steam can escape during cooking (or the cake will turn into a stew). Cook in oven for 1 hour, reduce temperature to 160°C (315°F/Gas 2–3) (140°C/275°F fan forced), remove foil and cook for another hour. Test with a skewer; it should come out clean. If too wet, cook a bit longer. Remove from oven, let cool, place a piece of baking paper on top and a plate to weigh down cake and refrigerate overnight.

Next day, turn cake out onto a large serving plate. Be aware of the juices. Remove baking paper carefully so sultanas remain intact. Cut and serve, hot or warm, with juices on top and crème anglaise.

For crème anglaise, in a small saucepan bring milk and cinnamon to the boil. Whisk egg yolks with Equal in a heatproof bowl until pale. Pour hot milk into egg mixture, whisking constantly. Return mixture to pan and stir constantly with a wooden spoon over low heat until custard thickens enough to coat the back of the spoon. Strain and keep aside.

DIETITIAN TIP
If you use skim milk, this recipe is low in fat. It's also very high in fibre.

NIP
Energy   807 kJ (193 Cal)
Total fat   2 g
Saturated fat   0.7 g
Carbohydrate   34 g

BLUEBERRY TART

JANNI KYRITSIS

Blueberry compote is one of the simplest and most delicious recipes. It can be served on its own or with other mixed berries and a spoonful of yoghurt. In this recipe, I use it as a topping for a blueberry tart. If you happen to have six small fluted tart (flan) tins, you can use half a filo pastry sheet, folded in half for extra strength. With individual flans it makes it easier to assemble and serve without worrying that the pastry will fall to pieces.

I have adapted the classic pastry cream and made it lighter with the addition of egg whites. Normally it is cooked with ¼ cup (55 g/2 oz) sugar and, when cold, ¾ cup (185 ml/6 fl oz) whipped cream is added.

1 tbsp melted butter

3 sheets filo pastry

whipped cream, to serve (optional)

BLUEBERRY COMPOTE

300 g (10½ oz) blueberries

zest of ¼ lemon

2 tsp lemon juice

2 tbsp Equal

PASTRY CREAM

1 cup (250 ml/9 fl oz) milk

1 tsp natural vanilla extract

3 egg yolks

3 tbsp Equal

¼ cup (35 g/1¼ oz) plain (all-purpose) flour

2 egg whites

SERVES 6

Preheat oven to 200°C (400°F/Gas 6). Lightly brush a 22-cm (8½-in) fluted loose-based tart (flan) tin with butter.

Brush a 25-cm (10-in) circle in the centre of a sheet of filo pastry with butter, place another sheet of pastry on top and brush again with butter, place next sheet on top and brush again with butter. Lift pastry into tin and carefully push into fluted side, then cut excess pastry with scissors, leaving about 5 mm (¼ in) above rim of tin. With a fork, prick pastry many times so it will not puff up during cooking. Bake for about 5 minutes or until golden brown. Set aside to cool.

For blueberry compote, in a small saucepan, combine one-third of the blueberries, the lemon zest and juice and Equal, and bring to the boil for a few seconds. Fold in remaining blueberries, remove them to a bowl and leave in fridge to macerate for a couple of hours.

For pastry cream, combine milk and vanilla in a saucepan and bring to the boil. Whisk egg yolks with 2 tablespoons Equal until pale. Sift flour over egg yolk mixture and mix well (it will end up rather stiff).

Slowly pour hot milk and vanilla into egg mixture, whisking constantly to make sure there are no lumps. Return mixture to pan and stir over low heat until it just comes to a simmer. Reduce heat to very low and continue stirring for 4 minutes to cook out flour. Remove from heat and stir for 1 minute more. Transfer pastry cream to a bowl and stir occasionally while you prepare meringue. Whisk egg whites to soft peaks, slowly add last tablespoon of Equal and whisk to stiff peaks. Stir pastry cream again to make sure it has not set and is still warm. Fold in a quarter of the meringue and stir well, lightly fold in the rest, and refrigerate until you're ready to serve.

To serve, carefully spoon pastry cream into pastry shell and top with blueberry compote. Remove side of tin, and cut tart into 6 portions. Serve immediately or pastry will lose its crispness. A spoonful of whipped cream, if desired, goes well with it.

DIETITIAN TIP
By using filo pastry, Janni has kept the fat content to a minimum.

NIP

Energy	648 kJ (155 Cal)
Total fat	7 g
Saturated fat	4 g
Carbohydrate	17 g

APPLE AND PASSIONFRUIT JELLY WITH FRESH PINEAPPLE AND PASSIONFRUIT

ANN OLIVER

almond or apricot oil, for oiling moulds

600 ml (21 fl oz) cold apple and passionfruit juice (I use Preshafruit)

12 g (¼ oz) gold-strength gelatine sheet

1 small sugar pineapple, peeled and cut into small cubes

pulp of 2 passionfruit

SERVES 4

Lightly oil four 150-ml (5-fl oz) dariole moulds with almond or apricot oil.

Measure about 150 ml (5 fl oz) juice into a small saucepan and place over high heat. As soon as it comes to the boil, turn off heat.

Place gelatine in cold water with a few ice cubes, until it is softened (about 3 minutes), squeeze out and stir into hot juice. Continue to stir until completely dissolved, then stir into remaining cold fruit juice to thoroughly combine. Divide between oiled moulds, place on a small tray or plate, cover with plastic wrap and refrigerate for at least 5 hours.

Unmould a jelly onto each plate. Mix pineapple dice and passionfruit pulp together, then divide between the jellies and serve.

NOTE: Try adding 1 tablespoon white wine vinegar and a pinch of sea salt to 2⅓ cups (580 ml/20¼ fl oz) Preshafruit granny smith apple juice and proceed in the same manner. Set in a single square-edged oiled mould and serve, cut into 2-cm (¾-in) squares, with chopped granny smith apples, shallot, celery and toasted walnuts, dressed with a tarragon mayonnaise. It's really fast and fabulous and gives a delicious and good-looking twist to the classic apple and celery salad.

DIETITIAN TIP
Another lovely recipe that uses gelatine to make fruit more interesting.

NIP

Energy	407 kJ (97 Cal)
Total fat	0.2 g
Saturated fat	NIL
Carbohydrate	21 g

CHERRY AND DARK CHOCOLATE MOUSSE TART

JANNI KYRITSIS

Here I'm using the chocolate mousse recipe to create a new dessert. I have used a very thin spread of chocolate as a base instead of the usual rich shortcrust pastry that is the most likely base for a tart. My first test failed miserably – I used only 50 g (1¾ oz) chocolate for the tart shell and when I tried to lift the wedge it broke. So what did I do? I broke it even more and served the mousse as spoonfuls on the plate. My guests thought it was a novel way to add flakes of chocolate through the mousse. Some of the best dishes are born out of disasters. The success of this dish depends on the quality of the cherries. Make sure you buy large ripe cherries. Kirsch is wonderful in bringing out the flavour of the cherries but you can use any alcohol of your choice.

1 kg (2 lb 4 oz) large cherries, pitted and cut in half, reserving about 16 to decorate

2 tbsp kirsch

125 g (4½ oz) dark chocolate (70 per cent cocoa solids), broken into pieces

4 extra large eggs (67 g/2½ oz each), at room temperature, separated

¼ cup (40 g/1½ oz) whole almonds

1 tsp icing (confectioners') sugar, for dusting (optional)

TART BASE

75 g (2½ oz) dark chocolate (70 per cent cocoa solids), broken into pieces

SERVES 8

Place cherry halves and kirsch in a saucepan, cover and bring to a simmer. Set aside to cool, then place in fridge until you are ready to assemble the tart. You want cherries to be just soft. Reserve 2 tablespoons cherry juice for mousse.

For tart base, melt chocolate in a heatproof bowl over a saucepan of simmering water. Slightly wet your kitchen bench and spread a piece of plastic wrap on it. Pour on melted chocolate and spread with a spatula to form a ring just big enough to cover base and side of a 22-cm (8½-in) fluted loose-based tart (flan) tin. You will need some help to lift chocolate-covered plastic wrap onto tin. With the help of a toothpick, ease plastic wrap into fluted side. Place in the fridge to harden. If all this is too technical, simply use a 22-cm (8½-in) springform cake tin, cut a piece of baking paper to fit, place in base of tin and spread chocolate over. (It will not look as attractive but it will taste the same.)

For chocolate mousse, combine chocolate pieces and reserved cherry juice in a heat-proof bowl. Place bowl on top of a saucepan of simmering water and turn off heat. Let chocolate

melt undisturbed for about 10 minutes. Whisk egg whites to very soft peaks. In a separate bowl, whisk egg yolks for a moment and fold them into chocolate cherry mixture, then fold in egg whites. Stop folding as soon as egg white is incorporated.

When mousse is made, spread cold cherries over tart base in tin and pour mousse on top. Refrigerate for a few hours. It develops a better flavour if left overnight.

Preheat oven to 150°C (300°F/Gas 2).

Meanwhile, put almonds in boiling water for a couple of minutes, drain and rinse in cold water. Squeeze almonds out of their skins and toast in oven for 20 minutes, or until golden. Set aside to cool, then chop roughly and mix with icing sugar, if desired.

Remove side of tin and ease tart off plastic wrap or baking paper. Sprinkle chopped almonds over top and, with a hot knife, cut tart into 8 pieces. Using a cake knife, carefully lift wedges onto plates, decorate with reserved cherries and serve.

DIETITIAN TIP
A great recipe for a special occasion when the higher fat content can be ignored.

NIP Includes icing (confectioners') sugar

Energy	1195 kJ (286 Cal)
Total fat	13 g
Saturated fat	5 g
Carbohydrate	33 g

CARDAMOM YOGHURT PUDDING AND SAFFRON PEARS

JANNI KYRITSIS

You'd expect me to use Greek-style yoghurt for this recipe; however, I've found that the basic plain supermarket yoghurt works best. Different yoghurts have different setting points and acidities. If you feel the puddings have set too firmly, you can leave them to come to room temperature before serving. This yoghurt pudding can be flavoured with other herbs or spices such as rose geranium or vanilla.

Small corella pears are best for this dish. Stale cardamom powder can be unpleasant, so use only cardamom pods and remove the seeds and grind them yourself. Don't use any more than you need as it can be overpowering. If you decide to use vanilla only, double the quantity, or to your taste.

I served this pudding, flavoured with rose geranium leaves and accompanied by orange liqueur-macerated strawberries, for three years at the Hyde Park Food and Wine Fair for charity. It was so popular that we sold 500 serves within an hour every time. I have since then modified the recipe, making it lighter to suit my needs of today.

½ cup (125 ml/4 fl oz) milk

2 tsp powdered gelatine

600 g (1 lb 5 oz) plain no-fat yoghurt

½ tsp natural vanilla extract

⅛ tsp ground cardamom seeds (from about 3 pods)

2 tbsp Splenda, or other artificial sweetener to taste

1 egg white

SAFFRON PEARS

1 cup (250 ml/9 fl oz) clear pure unsweetened apple juice

1 cup (250 ml/9 fl oz) white wine

¼ tsp saffron threads

6 small pears, peeled, cored and halved lengthways

SERVES 6

Pour milk into a saucepan and sprinkle gelatine over it, then let it stand for a few minutes to soften. Heat over low heat until gelatine is dissolved, and set aside.

In a large bowl, combine yoghurt, vanilla, cardamom and sweetener and stir well. In another bowl, whisk egg white until just at soft peak stage. Add a quarter of the yoghurt to milk mixture and stir to combine. Stir this mixture into remaining yoghurt in bowl and fold in egg white.

Rinse six ½-cup (125-ml/4-fl oz) dariole moulds or coffee cups in cold water and shake to remove excess water. Divide yoghurt mixture between moulds, smooth tops and refrigerate for a few hours or overnight.

For saffron pears, bring apple juice, wine and saffron to the boil in a saucepan in which pears just fit. Place pears in pan, bring to a simmer, reduce heat, cover with a piece of baking paper cut to fit pan and cook just below simmering for about 20 minutes, or until pears are tender. Refrigerate in pan for a few hours but preferably overnight.

One or two hours before serving, remove pears from pan, bring poaching liquid to the boil and reduce to ½ cup (125 ml/4 fl oz). Set aside to get cold.

To serve, place each mould in hot water for a moment and, with the help of a knife, carefully unmould pudding onto a serving plate. Place 2 pear halves on each plate, drizzle syrup over them and serve.

DIETITIAN TIP
Another good example of providing a serve of fruit and dairy in the same recipe.

NIP

Energy	725 kJ (173 Cal)
Total fat	1 g
Saturated fat	0.8 g
Carbohydrate	26 g

EDAMAME SNOW DRIFT
HIDEO DEKURA

60 g (2¼ oz) fresh or frozen edamame (green soya beans), cooked and shelled (see notes)

2 tsp maple syrup

1½ cups (375 ml/13 fl oz) water

1 tsp agar-agar soaked in ½ cup (125 ml/ 4 fl oz) water for 15 minutes (see notes)

1 egg white

1 tsp caster (superfine) sugar

pomegranate seeds or strawberries, to decorate

SERVES 2

Place edamame, maple syrup and water in a blender and whiz until smooth. Transfer to a saucepan and bring to the boil. Remove from heat, stir in agar-agar mixture and cook over low heat while mixing well to dissolve. Pour into individual serving glasses and set aside in fridge for 1 hour, or until set.

To make meringue, beat egg white in a bowl until soft peaks form. Beat in sugar until thick and glossy.

To serve, top jelly with meringue and pomegranate seeds or strawberries.

NOTES: Frozen edamame are available in Asian grocery shops.

Agar-agar is a setting agent made from seaweed.

DIETITIAN TIP
What a unique way to use legumes, and this is very low in kilojoules.

NIP	WITH STRAWBERRY	WITH POMEGRANATE
Energy	219 kJ (52 Cal)	279 kJ (67 Cal)
Total fat	0.5 g	0.5 g
Saturated fat	NIL	NIL
Carbohydrate	8 g	11 g

CRÈME CARAMEL LUXE

TONY BILSON

300 g (10½ oz) caster (superfine) sugar

650 ml (22½ fl oz) thin (pouring) cream

350 ml (12 fl oz) milk

200 g (7 oz) sugar

1 vanilla bean, split in half lengthways

zest of ½ lemon

zest of ½ orange

1 cinnamon stick

6 cardamom pods

4 egg yolks

4 eggs

SERVES 12

Melt caster sugar in a heavy-bottomed, stainless steel saucepan over a high heat, stirring constantly until caramelised, about 2 minutes. You must watch the sugar constantly and remove from heat as soon as the desired degree of caramelisation is reached. I prefer a dark caramel. Cover base of twelve 200-ml (7-fl oz) stainless steel dariole moulds with 2 mm (¹⁄₁₆ in) of caramel.

Preheat oven to 120°C (235°F/Gas ½).

Place cream, milk, sugar, vanilla bean, lemon and orange zest, cinnamon and cardamom in a saucepan and bring to the boil, stirring all the time. Remove from heat and leave for 5 minutes to infuse the flavours.

Combine egg yolks and eggs in a heatproof bowl and blend with a hand-held blender. Add hot milk mixture through a fine strainer, blend into eggs then pass through a fine strainer into a jug. Pour over caramel in moulds to within 2 cm (¾ in) of top.

Have a baking dish ready with 3 cm (1¼ in) boiling water in it to make a bain-marie (water bath). Place filled moulds in bain-marie and bake for 30 minutes, or until custard mixture has set. Refrigerate and, when cold, cover with plastic wrap to prevent dehydration.

NOTE: This method of preparing the custard with the hot sweetened milk makes for a finer, richer set.

DIETITIAN TIP
Saving a very special recipe, Amanda and Tony's indulgent treat, for last.

NIP Based on 1 tsp
caramel per mould
Energy   1365 kJ (326 Cal)
Total fat   23 g
Saturated fat   14 g
Carbohydrate   23 g

CONTRIBUTORS' BIOGRAPHIES

STEPHANIE ALEXANDER established her reputation as a restaurateur, owning and operating important Melbourne restaurants for more than 30 years. She is the best-selling author of 14 books, including The Cook's Companion, regarded as an Australian classic. In 2004 she established the Stephanie Alexander Kitchen Garden Foundation, a not-for-profit organisation of which she is now a director and Board member. Stephanie was the recipient of an Order of Australia in 1994.

JONATHAN BARTHELMESS landed his first head chef position at only 21. At Coast, he was able to draw on his Greek heritage and firmly establish his true passion for Mediterranean flavours, receiving a coveted Chef Hat from the Sydney Morning Herald Good Food Guide 2007. In 2009, the Italian edition of Gourmet Traveller magazine nominated Jonathan as the best new talent.

MAGGIE BEER is a self-taught cook, writer, ex-restaurateur and food producer based in South Australia's Barossa Valley. She co-hosted the successful cooking show The Cook and the Chef with Simon Bryant. Maggie won the Best Regional Cookbook in the World Cookbook Awards for Maggie's Table and she was named 2010's Senior Australian of the Year.

SHANNON BENNETT has trained under some of the world's finest chefs. In 2000, he established Vue de monde in Melbourne. His philosophy is to create food that would be close to impossible to cook at home. Australian Gourmet Traveller named him Best New Talent in 2004 and since then, it's been awards and Three Chef Hats every year.

TONY BILSON, known as the 'Godfather of Australian Cuisine', has dedicated his life to the pursuit of excellence in gastronomy. He has been recognised as one of Australia's leading chefs for over 40 years and his restaurants have been milestones in the advance of Australian gastronomy. In 2007 Tony was honoured with an award for professional excellence by the Sydney Morning Herald Good Food Guide, acknowledging his contribution as a chef and restaurateur.

GEORGE BIRON's Sunnybrae Restaurant, near Birregurra in South Western Victoria, has been the setting for legendary lunches showcasing the best of regional food for over 20 years. He also presents hands-on cooking classes, which are followed by similarly legendary lunches. George not only teaches how to cook the dishes available in his restaurant but also grows most of his produce onsite. In 2001 he was inducted as a Melbourne Food & Wine Festival Legend.

MARTIN BOETZ's unique spin on Thai and Southern Chinese cooking has redefined modern Asian cuisine. In 1999 Martin joined forces with Sam Christie to launch Longrain Restaurant and Bar in Sydney's Surry Hills and Longrain in Melbourne. It is with this reputation and knowledge that he has published *Longrain Modern Thai Food*, and also developed a range of classic Thai sauces called Longrain Produce.

GUILLAUME BRAHIMI was born in Paris. His career includes working at the three-Michelin-star restaurant La Tour d'Argent and at Restaurant Jamin. In 2001 he took over the prestigious Guillaume at Bennelong in the Sydney Opera House. Guillaume also has Bistro Guillaume both in Melbourne and in Perth's Crown Entertainment Complex.

JACOB BROWN grew up with a love of cooking but, having done an apprenticeship in New Zealand, resisted joining the profession at first. When he joined the team at Sean's Panaroma, he finally stopped resisting his destiny. Stints at Bennelong, working under Janni Kyritsis, and Fuel followed. Jacob now runs his own restaurant, The Larder, in Wellington, New Zealand.

DANY CHOUET arrived from Paris in 1969 and started the French bistro Upstairs before going solo with Au Chabrol in Darlinghurst; both were outstanding successes. She opened Cleopatra in the Blue Mountains in 1984, and was awarded Two Hats in the *Sydney Morning Herald Good Food Guide* for 16 years in a row. She returned to South West France in 2000, and published her memoir, *So French*, in 2010.

SEAN CORKERY started his apprenticeship at Coast Restaurant before working at Fuel Bistro. After three years in London, he became sous chef at Sydney's Civic Hotel. In 2006 Sean moved to Café Sopra at Fratelli Fresh and in 2008 he opened Café Sopra at Potts Point. He was awarded a Chef's Hat in the 2012 *Sydney Morning Herald Good Food Guide* for Café Sopra in Waterloo. In 2012 Sean was head chef at Rowley Leigh's Le Café Anglais in London. He is now running the kitchen at the One-Chef-Hat Café Sopra in Bridge Street, Sydney.

SERGE DANSEREAU started work in Sydney at The Regent in 1983. He spent eighteen years at the hotel, gaining their flagship restaurant Three Chef Hats. He explores overseas trends and encourages a greater knowledge of what we can produce in Australia. Serge is now the head chef and owner of the iconic Bathers' Pavilion in Balmoral Beach, where he has been since 1998.

HIDEO DEKURA, Master of the Japanese Master Chef Association, was born in Tokyo. After years of cooking and demonstrating in Japan, Hideo's interests led him to Europe to study classical French cuisine. In 1974 he settled in Sydney, where he now runs his own catering company, Culinary Studio Dekura. In 2007 the Japanese government awarded Hideo the Award for Service to Japanese Food Culture.

KEVIN DONOVAN and his wife Gail operated the former Jean-Jacques restaurant in St Kilda as The Pavilion before they transformed it into Donovans. In 2000 they received the *Age Good Food Guide* award for Professional Excellence, and in 2001 Donovans was inducted into the American Express Hall of Fame for winning the Best Restaurant in Victoria award for three consecutive years.

GREG DOYLE was at the helm of Pier Restaurant for 21 years. He was awarded Restaurateur of the Year in 2007, and his restaurant Pier won '2008 National Restaurant of the Year' at the Gourmet Traveller Restaurant Awards, Three Chef Hats in the *Sydney Morning Herald Good Food Guide* and Three Stars in the *Gourmet Traveller Restaurant Guide*. Pier was also voted in the San Pellegrino Top 100 Restaurants of the Year in 2008 and 2009. He now oversees The Sailors Club in the same location.

PETER DOYLE, widely regarded as a founding father of modern Australian cuisine, is head chef of est. He won the Professional Excellence award in the 2003 and 2011 *Sydney Morning Herald Good Food Guide* Awards, and was Restaurateur of the Year at the Restaurant & Catering Awards in 2004. est. has earned the prestigious Three Chef Hats in the coveted *Good Food Guide* Awards since 2003, and was awarded 'Restaurant of the Year' in 2006 as well as 'Favourite Modern Australian'.

RODNEY DUNN, the founder of The Agrarian Kitchen, was a former full-time food editor at *Australian Gourmet Traveller*. Raised in Griffith, in southern central New South Wales, he left home for the city to pursue his interest in cooking, working in restaurants such as Tetsuya's. In 2007 Rodney and his wife Séverine Demanet left Sydney and settled in Lachlan in the Derwent Valley, Tasmania. The Agrarian Kitchen opened in late 2008.

MANU FEILDEL's first job was at The Cafe Royal in London. In 1999 he flew to Melbourne and worked at Toofey's before heading to Sydney where he worked at Hugo's, Hugo's Lounge, Restaurant VII and Bilson's. Manu now co-hosts *My Kitchen Rules* on Channel 7, and has opened his own restaurant, L'étoile, in Sydney's Paddington.

LUCIO GALLETTO OAM hails from a Ligurian family of restaurateurs. His first job in Sydney in 1977 was at Natalino's Restaurant in Kings Cross. Lucio's first appeared in Balmain in 1981, then it moved to Paddington in 1983. Lucio has proudly continued the family tradition of exceptional service. For him, the restaurant is also a reflection of his well known passion for art. Lucio's kitchen remains true to his motto: 'We follow the season, not the fashion'.

PETER GILMORE was inspired to cook by his mother, who took him along to a gas cooking class when he was only 4. Since 2001 Peter has been executive chef at Quay, where he has maintained Three Chef Hats in the *Sydney Morning Herald Good Food Guide* for ten consecutive years. Quay is currently ranked among the S Pellegrino World's Top 50 Restaurants and has been voted best restaurant in Australasia for the past three years.

GUY GROSSI is a renowned chef who owns and operates Mirka Continental Bistro, Merchant Osteria Veneta, Ombra Salumi Bar and the venerable Grossi Florentino. Guy's name is synonymous with Melbourne and quality dining, and he is well respected within the community as a mentor and philanthropist.

AARON HARVIE was in the final six of *MasterChef* 2010 and currently hosts his own cooking show, *Love to Share*, on Network Ten. Aaron's love of cooking began when he was a teenager, living in Queensland with his mum and stepfather. He is presently concentrating on a line of food products, including Mexican and Italian sauces and oils.

DETLEF HAUPT has extensive experience in kitchens throughout Germany, Switzerland, Asia and the Middle East, which led him to the role of executive chef of the Sydney Convention and Exhibition Centre. There he regularly turned Australian produce into exquisite meals for some 5000 guests. With a motto of 'quality and quantity', he maintains that catering for 1000 should be no different than catering for ten.

DAMIAN HEADS specialises in modern Australian cuisine, with a focus on fresh produce being prepared on an open wood-fired grill. Damian was awarded the Josephine Pignolet Award for Best Young Chef in 2001. Damian spends most of his time in the kitchens between his restaurants, while also managing to participate in cooking demonstrations, provide cooking classes and cater for private parties.

DANIEL HONG, winner of the Josephine Pignolet Best Young Chef of the Year 2007, began cooking professionally about six years ago. After his apprenticeships at Longrain, Pello and Marque restaurants, Daniel worked for a short time at world-acclaimed Tetsuya's in Sydney and also at Bentley Restaurant & Bar as sous chef. Daniel is now executive chef at three Merivale establishments – Ms. G's, El Loco and Mr. Wong.

BELINDA JEFFERY is a chef, food writer, television presenter and the author of several cookbooks. At the age of 10 she was inspired by Margaret Fulton's first big cookbook. Belinda's passion is making the heart and soul recipes that you find in old country cookbooks.

PHILIP JOHNSON honed his skills in Australia, London and New Zealand before settling in Brisbane. He opened his landmark bistro, e'cco, in 1995 and very quickly made a name for himself with his win of the 1997 Remy Martin Cognac/*Australian Gourmet Traveller* Restaurant of the Year Award. He has continued to receive national and international acclaim for his flair and elegant simplicity. Philip has also written six cookbooks.

JENNICE KERSH and RAYMOND KERSH, who ran the award-winning restaurant Edna's Table until 2005, have been creating and serving native Australian cuisine for 30 years, using ingredients such as wallaby, kangaroo, emu and crocodile alongside warrigal greens, samphire, lemon myrtle, cheese, Davidson plum, fruit, wattleseed and other treasures of the bush.

KYLIE KWONG has written many books sharing the wonderful home cooking that nourished her as a child. As well as running her own restaurant, Billy Kwong, Kylie has appeared in two TV series, *Kylie Kwong: Heart and Soul* and *My China*. Kylie is a firm believer that our food choices should be ethical, sustainable and supportive of both the natural and human environment.

JANNI KYRITSIS learned his culinary skills at the hands of Stephanie Alexander in Melbourne, then with Gay Bilson at Berowra Waters Inn. Janni went on to cook at Bennelong at the Sydney Opera House, and opened the innovative MG Garage, earning Three Chef Hats in his first year. He left the full-time restaurant business in 2002 but will never stop cooking.

CHUI LEE LUK was born in Singapore. After qualifying as a lawyer, Chui realised her calling was not to practise law but to cook. Her innate understanding of South East Asian, Chinese and French cuisines gives her a unique culinary insight. In 2004 she took over as the owner and chef at Claude's Woollahra.

ADAM LIAW was the 2010 *MasterChef* winner. His inspiration for cooking began in his grandmother's kitchen in Adelaide. Adam's love affair with food really blossomed during the six years he lived in Japan. The author of *Two Asian Kitchens*, Adam is an ambassador for Malaysian Kitchen, a year-long event to promote the food from his country of origin.

CHEONG LIEW was born in Malaysia. His creative cuisine has been called daring, and he was honoured by the prestigious *American Food and Wine* magazine as 'one of the 10 hottest chefs alive'. Cheong was awarded the Medal of the Order of Australia in the 1999 Queen's Birthday Honours for services to the food and restaurant industry.

ANDREW McCONNELL has worked in London and Asia. He returned to Melbourne to open Diningroom 211, where he shared the 2002 Young Chef of the Year prize with his brother Matthew. He currently owns Cumulus Inc., Cutler & Co., Golden Fields and the Builders Arms Hotel with dining room Moon Under Water.

CHRISTINE MANFIELD is one of Australia's most celebrated chefs. A perfectionist inspired by strong flavours, Chris is a creative spirit whose generosity and skills have inspired many young chefs. She is a successful writer, restaurateur, presenter and teacher, and her culinary work draws on the exciting tastes and flavours of many cultures.

STEFANO MANFREDI is an Italian-born chef, author and leading exponent of modern Italian cuisine in Australia. He has opened and operated several restaurants since 1983, most notably Restaurant Manfredi, Bel Mondo and Manfredi at Bells, where he took the helm in 2007. His latest restaurant, Balla, opened at The Star Casino in Sydney in 2011. He has written on food and cooking since 1988, is a regular columnist for the *Sydney Morning Herald* and is the author of four books.

LUKE MANGAN currently owns and operates glass brasserie, Hilton Sydney; Salt grill, Hilton Surfers Paradise; Salt grill and Salt tapas & bar, Singapore; Salt and the adjoining World Wine Bar, Tokyo; and Salt grill on board three P&O cruise liners. The consulting chef for Virgin Australia, Luke has written four best-selling cookbooks as well as his autobiography, *The Making of a Chef*. In addition he has launched his own range of gourmet products.

MICHAEL MANNERS established Selkirks Restaurant in Orange in 1997, following successful stints in the Blue Mountains, Sydney and Europe. Selkirks developed a national reputation for its innovative and beautiful food, welcoming atmosphere and commitment to premium local produce. Michael is now semi-retired and catering for small functions and a pop-up restaurant, Chapter 2, with Kate Bracks in the Hardback Cafe in Orange.

GARY MEHIGAN has trained in world-class restaurants such as The Connaught and Le Souffle in London. Since 1991 Gary has been based in Melbourne, where he has headed the kitchens in prominent restaurants, including Browns and Hotel Sofitel. In 2000 Gary opened his own award-winning restaurant, Fenix, and is now also one of the hosts of *MasterChef Australia*.

Food and wine personality LYNDEY MILAN's no-nonsense approach has built her a solid career on television, radio and in print. Her latest cookbook, *Lyndey and Blair's Taste of Greece* accompanies the critically acclaimed television series of the same name – co-hosted with her late son, Blair – which has been sold around the world. She has been a *Good Food Guide* reviewer since 1987. In 2012 her peers awarded her The Vittoria Legend Award.

MATT MORAN is the executive chef and co-owner of awarded ARIA restaurant in Sydney. In 2009 he opened a second ARIA restaurant in Brisbane, and in 2012 CHISWICK in Woollahra, where much of the produce for the menu is grown in the kitchen garden, the heart of the restaurant. While Matt's main focus remains his restaurants, he regularly contributes to various TV shows, magazines and newspapers, and is the author of three best-selling cookbooks.

SEAN MORAN has had a long and distinguished career, and has worked with some of Australia's most talented chefs, including Gay Bilson, Janni Kyritsis, Anders Ousback, Neil Perry and Stefano Manfredi, before opening his own restaurant, Sean's Panaroma, in 1993. Approaching its 20th anniversary, Sean's beachside restaurant continues to garner local, national and international acclaim.

ROBERTA MUIR's passion for food, wine and foreign culture has led her on adventures around the world. Since 1997 she has managed Sydney Seafood School at Sydney Fish Market, one of Australia's leading cooking schools. A reviewer for the Australian *Gourmet Traveller Restaurant Guide*, she is also the author of the *Sydney Seafood School Cookbook* (2012) and *500 Cheeses* (2010) and co-author, with chef Giovanni Pilu, of *A Sardinian Cookbook*.

LAUREN MURDOCH began training at Atlas Bistro in Riley Street and moved to Rockpool for a year's pastry experience before working at the Concourse Restaurant at the Sydney Opera House. Janni Kyritsis made Lauren his sous chef when he opened MG Garage in 1997. In 2005, she accepted the offer to run the kitchen at Lotus Bistro in Potts Point. Lauren's last restaurant gig was at Felix. She now runs her own business.

ANN OLIVER has spent 33 years cooking at the highest level and her passion remains undiminished. A lifetime association with producers who share her obsession for seasonal food grown under sustainable circumstances has had a profound effect on the food she cooks and writes about.

TIM PAK POY trained in Adelaide under chef Cheong Liew. Pak Poy moved to Sydney, where he owned and operated the celebrated Claude's Restaurant and the Wharf at Sydney Theatre Company. Pak Poy's consultancy currently develops food concepts and operations for the hospitality industry.

ALESSANDRO PAVONI began his career in Brescia, northern Italy. He has worked in Michelin-starred venues such as Rotonde in Lyon, France, and the Villa Fiordaliso on Lake Garda, Italy. In 2009 he opened his own restaurant, Ormeggio at The Spit, in Mosman, Sydney. The restaurant provides a contemporary Italian experience in an Australian harbourside setting.

ARMANDO PERCUOCO has worked in restaurants for most of his life, starting in his family's restaurant in Naples. He came to Australia in 1972 and, with his father, opened Pulcinella in Kings Cross in 1979. In 1987 he opened Buon Ricordo, offering unpretentious dishes with an emphasis on flavour and taste. Armando was instrumental in establishing the 'Five Chefs Dinner' for the Starlight Foundation, raising money for seriously ill children.

NEIL PERRY is one of Australia's leading and most influential chefs. By the time he was 24, he had realised his passion for cooking. He opened Rockpool in 1989. In 2006 he opened Rockpool Bar and Grill in the Crown Complex in Melbourne. Neil now owns seven award-winning restaurants in Sydney, Melbourne and Perth. In 2013 Neil was awarded an AM in the Honours List for his services to the restaurant industry and for his charity work.

DAMIEN PIGNOLET's career, which spans over 40 years, has involved catering, teaching cookery, opening restaurants and, in recent years, writing two books, *French* and *Salades*. Of his nine sydney restaurants he believes Claude's and Bistro Moncur to have been the best. Damien administers the prestigious Josephine Pignolet Best Young Chef of the Year Award, and now heads Paddington's Bellevue Hotel dining room as the executive chef.

GEORGE POMPEI is a master at his craft. He has the best gelateria outside of Napoli, while his pizzas impress with an emphasis on authentic flavour, and the pasta is house made. With a perfect location at Bondi Beach, it is possible to enjoy this artisan's craft at his eponymously named Pompei's.

MATT PRESTON is an internationally acclaimed food critic, well known for his cravats and warm on-screen presence. A seasoned journalist, he was awarded the title of World's Best Food Journalist in 2008 at the World Food Media Awards. Before joining *MasterChef Australia*, he was creative director of the Melbourne Food & Wine Festival for over five years.

DAVID PUGH grew up in Auckland, and his love of cooking started when he was 7. He is the owner and chef of Brisbane's Restaurant Two. David's professional experience includes working with a diverse range of talented chefs in some of the finest restaurants in the world. In 2009 he was appointed Queensland's Ambassador Chef to help promote the state's reputation for excellence, and in 2010 he represented Queensland at the Shanghai Expo.

BRENT SAVAGE has been acknowledged by both his peers and the food media as one of the most talented chefs in Australia. In 2006, with business partner and award-winning sommelier Nick Hildebrandt, he opened Bentley Restaurant & Bar, which has been awarded Two Chef Hats. In 2013 they opened Monopole, a celebrated wine bar in Potts Point. Nominated for numerous awards, Brent has received rave reviews in *Australian Gourmet Traveller* magazine.

CAROL SELVA RAJAH, one of Australia's most celebrated Asian cuisine experts, is the award-winning author of eleven cookbooks on South East Asian cooking. A celebrity chef who has been admitted to *The Sydney Magazine*'s Food Hall of Fame, in 1994 she became the first woman invited to cook at the James Beard Foundation in New York.

STEVEN SNOW is the internationally renowned owner and chef of Fins, Australia's most awarded regional restaurant. The author of two cookbooks, Steven has recently opened his second Fins, Fins Club by Quinta Magnolia in a small seaside village near Lisbon, Portugal. Away from the pans Steven was the feature chef on Channel 7's lifestyle program *Guide to the Good Life*.

JANE STRODE began her apprenticeship at Sydney's Rockpool. She then worked at Langton's and MG Garage with Jeremy before opening Bistrode with him in 2005. The Strodes achieved their first Chef Hat after only two years. The husband-and-wife team continue to strive for excellence with their second restaurant, Bistrode CBD, opened in 2010 with the Merivale Group.

JEREMY STRODE arrived in Melbourne from London in 1992 and was head chef at The George Hotel, the Aldelphi and his own restaurant Pomme and finally Langton's. In 2002 he headed to Sydney to become chef director of MG Garage. In 2005 he and wife Jane Strode opened Bistrode, where they achieved a Chef Hat for six consecutive years before its sale in 2012. In 2010 Jeremy opened Sydney's Bistrode CBD, and in 2012 The Fish Shop, both with the Merivale Group.

TETSUYA WAKUDA arrived in Sydney from Japan in 1983. He opened his eponymous restaurant in Rozelle in 1989, where he established a dedicated following. In 2000 the restaurant moved to Kent Street in Sydney's CBD. In 2010 Tetsuya opened his second restaurant, Waku Ghin, at Marina Bay Sands, Singapore.

CHRISTOPHER WHITEHEAD learned his trade with Gay Bilson and Janni Kyritsis at Berowra Waters Inn. He earned his first Chef Hat in 2002 for his exceptional efforts at Bond restaurant. For six years Christopher was the executive chef at the Opera Bar before his love and appreciation of the diversity and history of food led him to Mad Cow. He is now head chef at Palings Kitchen and Bar.

INDEX